Table of Contents

How to read a tab

Understanding Tab

Guitar tab, or tablature, stands out as a widely embraced method for notating guitar music. Its allure lies in the ease of reading once you've grasped its intricacies.

To delve into tab comprehension, envision the guitar neck as though you're poised to play, gazing down upon it. Tab comprises six horizontal lines mirroring the guitar strings, with the thickest string aligning at the bottom and the thinnest at the top.

The essence of Tab
Upon these lines, numbers denote finger placements on the guitar fretboard. In decoding the diagram below, executing it on the guitar involves positioning your finger just behind the 2nd fret on the 5th string, followed by playing the note at the 4th fret, and then revisiting the 2nd fret. The 'zero' signifies playing an open string. In the language of musical notes, this sequence translates to B, C#, B, A.

Guitar Tab Chords

Tabbing a chord involves aligning the notes in a vertical line along the horizontal ones. Illustrated here is a C Chord. To properly interpret this tab, a single sweeping motion should be employed to strum the bottom 5 strings of the guitar.

In this particular instance, the 'C Chord' is to be strummed thrice:

Hammer-On

Executing a hammer-on involves plucking a note and then forcefully pressing down with the fretting hand on the second note. Notably, the second note is not plucked but resonates as an echo of the first. In tab notation, hammer-ons are depicted as follows:

Pull-Off

Pull-offs, conversely, entail playing the first note again and then smoothly lifting the finger off with the fretting hand, allowing the one behind it to sound. The tab representation for pull-offs is structured as follows:

Bends

When the fretting hand induces a string to bend, producing a distinctive wobbling effect, it introduces what is known as a bend. This technique is commonly employed in solos and is tabbed in the following manner:

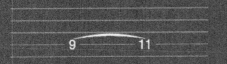

Release Bend

A release bend is akin to a standard bend, but it specifies the moment to ease off the bend and transition to the subsequent note.

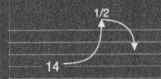

Slide

As for a slide, the process commences with plucking the initial note and smoothly transitioning along the string either upward or downward to reach the second note. In the provided tab, the sequence involves playing the first note on the 10th fret and subsequently sliding the finger maintaining that note down to the 8th fret (a slide-down):

In this scenario, a slide-up is executed by smoothly transitioning the finger from the 3rd fret to the 5th without lifting it:

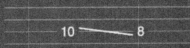

Legato Slide

In this context, the slide mirrors the conventional approach, with the distinction that the second note is not plucked, adhering to the typical slide technique.

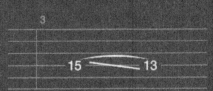

Slight Left Hand Vibrato

Vibrato introduces a constant rhythmic modulation of the string. This entails a swift upward and downward bending, generating a dynamic, oscillating sound. Slight Left Hand Vibrato is depicted in tab notation as follows:

Wide Left Hand Vibrato

To achieve a more pronounced pitch variation, the fretting hand employs a wider vibrato, which is tabbed as:

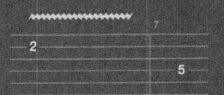

Vibrato w/ Trem. Bar

Utilizing the tremolo bar constitutes another method for inducing vibrato. If a beat encompasses multiple notes, this effect is applied uniformly to all the chord's notes. The Wide vibrato, in comparison to the Slight one, imparts a more noticeable and expansive modulation.

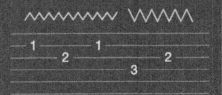

Let ring

The "Let ring" directive instructs you to sustain the note until the conclusion of the dashed line. In tab notation, it appears as follows:

Palm Mute

Creating a palm mute effect involves using the side of your right hand (the fourth finger side) to lightly touch the string at the bridge's edge. This imparts a muted quality to the played notes.

Ghost Note

A ghost note is best described as a note that is felt but not heard distinctly. It is played softer, lacking emphasis, and can be executed by fretting a note without picking it. Ghost notes, symbolized by round brackets in notation, contribute subtly to the musical ambiance, adding nuance to the overall feel.

Dead Note

A dead note involves muting the strings using your left hand, achieved by lightly resting your left hand across the strings without applying pressure against the fret. The tab notation for a dead note appears as follows:

Up/Down Strokes

For a sequence of chords, the playing technique is specified with downstrokes, upstrokes, or a combination. In tab notation, the direction of strokes is denoted as follows:

Up/Down Arpeggios

When employing the arpeggio technique, chords are played with rapid succession, allowing the individual notes within the chord to be heard distinctly. Up/Down Arpeggios are tabbed as follows:

Natural Harmonics

Natural harmonics produce a bell-like resonance when a string is touched over a specific fret bar. The commonly used notation features the fret to be touched, preceded by a rhombus sign.

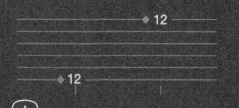

Polyphony

Polyphony, a musical texture comprising two or more independent lines of melody playing simultaneously, is represented in tabs. One of these lines is depicted in gray, indicating the fret number, while the other is shown in black.

Pinch Harmonic

A pinch harmonic, a guitar technique for creating artificial harmonics, involves the player's thumb or index finger on the picking hand slightly catching the string that was plucked. This action suppresses the fundamental frequency of the string, allowing one of the harmonics to take precedence.

Rhythm Notation

Tabs exclusively convey information about the pitch of notes and lack details about rhythm or note durations. Consequently, a tab can be played in various ways. While platforms like Songsterr provide the ability to visualize and audibly experience the tab as it's played, incorporating rhythm notation offers precise instructions on when to play a note and how long to sustain it. Rhythm notation closely resembles traditional sheet music notation (scores). Below, the fundamentals of rhythm notation are elucidated.

The Beat

Music is inherently bound by time, with a recurring pulse known as the beat forming the rhythmic foundation. This beat serves as a steady rhythm, inviting foot taps or dance moves. Visualize any music from a dance club, and the beat becomes immediately apparent—the constant element of time around which the music revolves.

Bars

To maintain structure in music, beats are organized into bars, also known as measures, each demarcated by bar lines. Typically, many songs comprise four beats per bar. The rhythmic cadence follows a sequential count: 4 ,3 ,2 ,1 ,4 ,3 ,2 ,1, and so forth, with beat one always signaling the onset of a new bar.

Time Signature

In tab notation, the time signature at the beginning of each tab serves as a guide. This fraction, with the top number representing the beats per bar (often 4), and the bottom number indicating the note value equivalent to each beat (usually 4), establishes the rhythmic framework. In essence, a time signature like 4/4 denotes that each bar encompasses four quarter notes, defining the pulse of the music.

Notes and Rests

Rhythm notation involves modifying the appearance of notes to signify their relative duration within a tab, while rests indicate the corresponding periods of silence. The nomenclature of notes and rests stems from their fractional value in relation to what constitutes a beat:

	NOTE	REST
Whole	(not signet)	▬
Half		▬
Quater		⸹
Eighth	⌐	⸾
Sixteenth	⌐	⸾
Thirty-Second	⌐	⸾

Basic rhythmic values are essentially simple fractions of the 4-beat whole note. Consider the rhythm notation in the tab below:

In this illustration, each note carries the value of a quarter, lasting one beat each. The tempo at which you play the tab can vary, but the relative duration remains consistent (one note for one beat). Another instance:

D5

All rhythm values can be derived from combining two values, each half the duration of the other:

Here, a pause with a duration of half (equivalent to two beats) precedes the repetition of the D5 chord played four times, each with an eighth note duration (half of a beat).

Beams

Smaller-valued notes are often grouped together using beams, with grouped notes typically spanning the length of one beat. It's noteworthy that rests are never beamed:

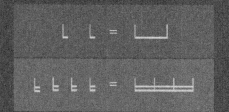

Dotted note

Additionally, notes and rests may be accompanied by a small dot, positioned just to the right of the rhythmic element. This dot extends the duration of the note or rest by one half.

Double-dotted note

The first dot elongates the note's duration by half, and the second dot further extends it by another quarter of the already elongated duration, equivalent to half of the preceding half.

Ties

Notes' durations can be extended through the use of ties. When tied, the following notes are sustained for the duration of the second note. It's important to note that rests are never tied together.

Grace-note before the beat

In musical notation, a grace note serves as an ornament, involving a swift note played just before another note. A grace note doesn't contribute to the bar's duration or rhythm display.

Grace-note on the beat

Similar to the grace note occurring just before the beat, one initiated precisely on the beat introduces a subtle delay in the onset of the subsequent beat.

Triplets

A triplet typically comprises three notes, collectively holding the duration of two notes of the same length when played. In the given example, notes are grouped in threes, where the duration of three of the triplet's eighth notes equals the duration of only one quarter note (not 8/3). Instead of dividing the quarter note by 2 to obtain eighth notes, it's divided by three. In standard music notation, these triplets usually have a '3' written underneath the group.

Swing Rhythm

In swing rhythm, the pulse is unevenly divided, with certain subdivisions (often eighth or sixteenth note subdivisions) alternating between long and short durations.

Repeats

The repeat sign in tab notation can be perplexing. When a pair of dots accompanies a double bar, it indicates that you must repeat the music either from the very beginning of the piece or from the previous repeat symbol, as follows:

In tab notation, it's crucial to follow the correct interpretation of repeat symbols. When you encounter repeat symbols with dots on the right side for the first time, disregard them. However, upon reaching a repeat symbol with dots on the left side, it signals that you should backtrack to the previous repeat symbol facing the opposite direction. In the absence of a previous symbol, return to the beginning of the piece. On subsequent encounters with the repeat symbol, ignore it unless it contains specific instructions like "3x" (indicating a repeat three times).

Alternate Endings

Sections often incorporate distinct endings after each repeat. For example, consider the illustration below, featuring a first and a second ending. Follow these steps: play until you encounter the first repeat symbol, then jump back to the previous repeat symbol (not shown in the picture). Continue playing until you reach the bracketed first ending, skip the measures beneath the bracket, immediately proceed to the second ending, and then resume playing.

Accented

An accented note calls for emphasis, a heightened attack on a specific note. Play this note louder than the others to highlight its significance.

Heavily accented

A heavily accented note demands maximum emphasis, an even more pronounced attack on a particular note. Play this note much louder than the others to create a distinctive impact.

Staccato

Staccato notation signals a very short note, regardless of the note's duration on the score. It directs the player to produce a brief and detached sound.

Popping

Popping is a technique commonly applied to bass guitars, involving a forceful plucking of one of the two highest strings using the right-hand index finger. This produces a sharp and percussive sound, adding a dynamic element to the music.

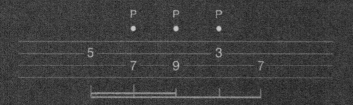

Slapping

Slapping is a technique predominantly employed on bass guitars. It entails the player hitting the strings with their right-hand thumb while rotating their wrist to generate a percussive sound. This technique adds rhythmic and percussive qualities to the bassline.

Tapping

Tapping involves striking a fret with your fingers without a preceding attack on the note, creating a distinct and often percussive sound.

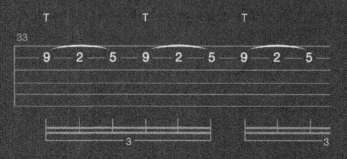

Tremolo

Tremolo is characterized by rapid, short picking motions both up and down. In this technique, the pick exerts the same force on the string during both downward and upward movements. The hand remains as relaxed as possible to achieve high speed and fluidity.

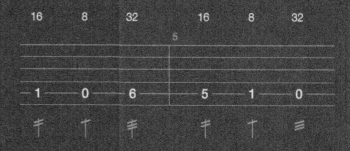

Anacrusis

Anacrusis, also known as a pickup bar or upbeat, is a partial or incomplete bar appearing at the beginning or end of a tab. This bar will not be marked as erroneous, even if it is left incomplete, providing flexibility in the representation of the musical passage.

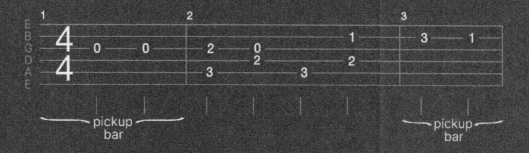

Taylor Swift
Love Story

Taylor Swift - Love Story

Track: Mike Meadows I - Acoustic Guitar (Nylon)

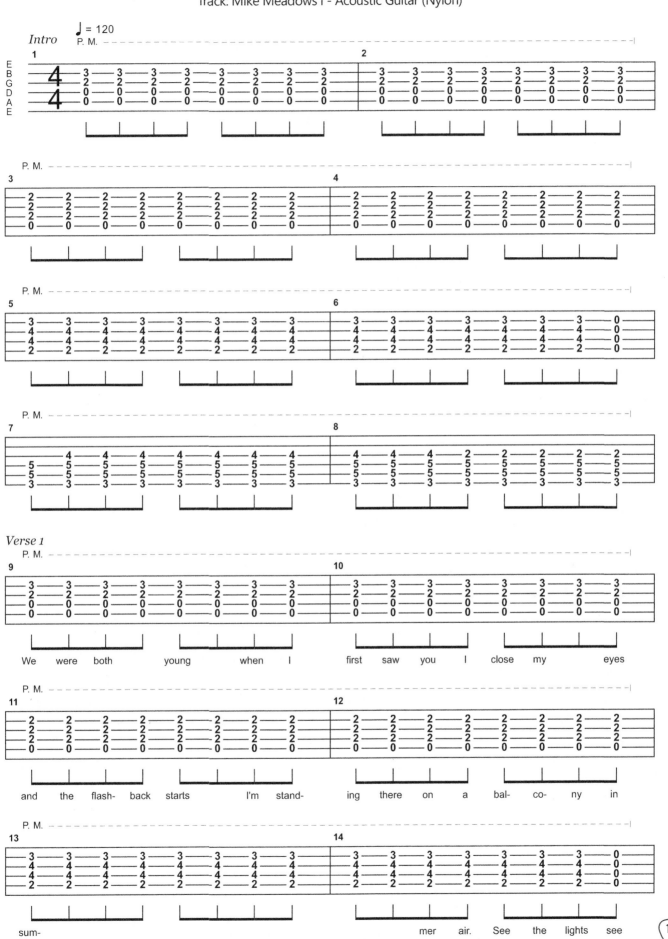

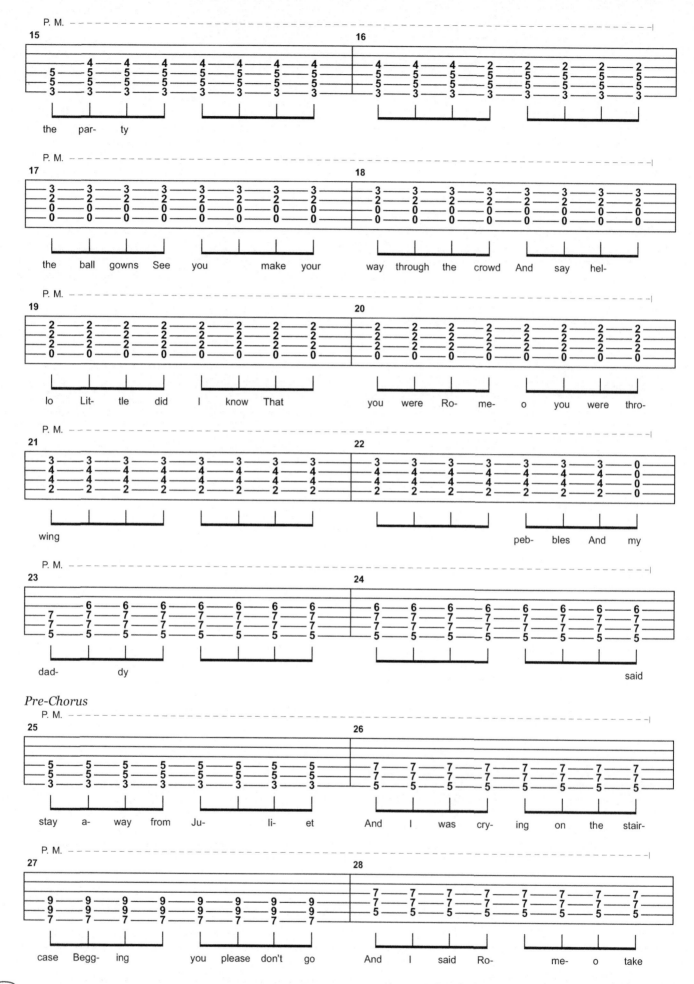

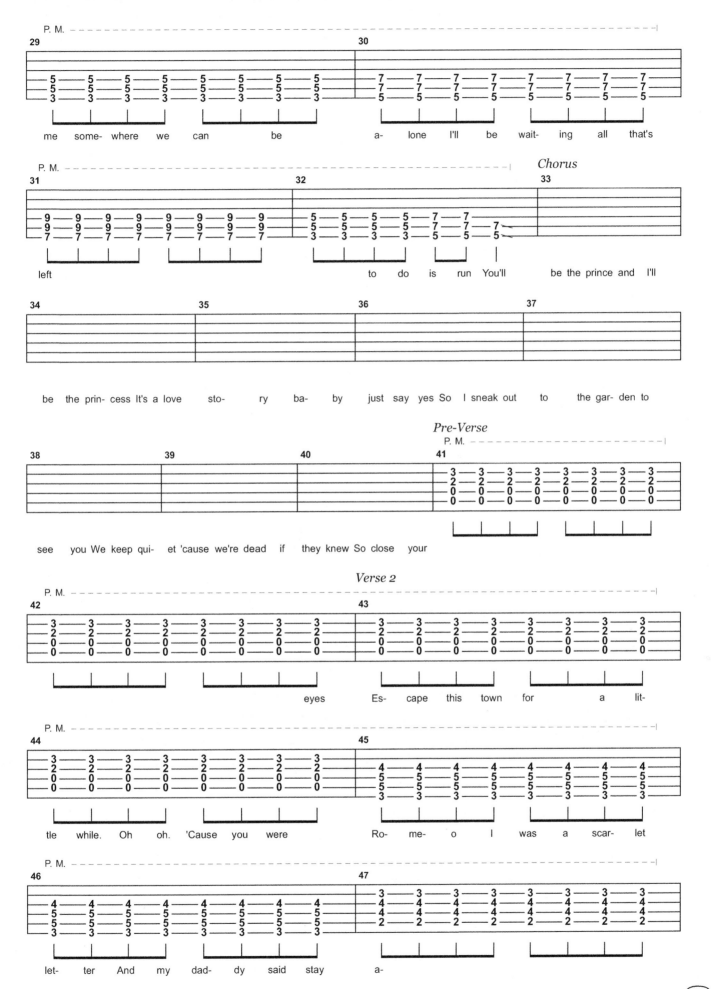

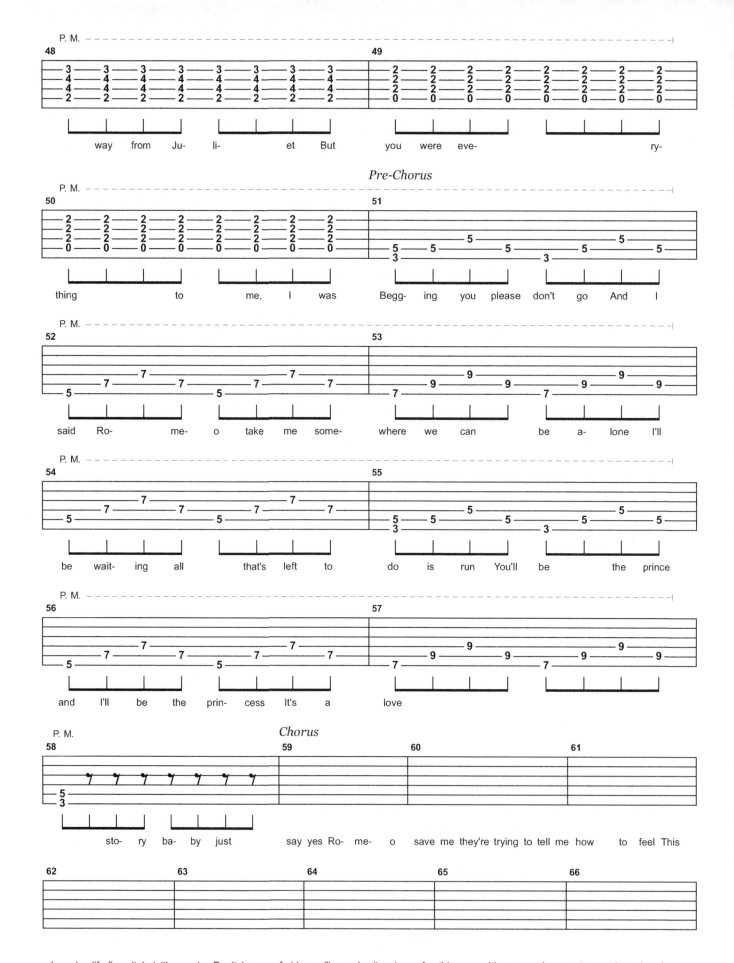

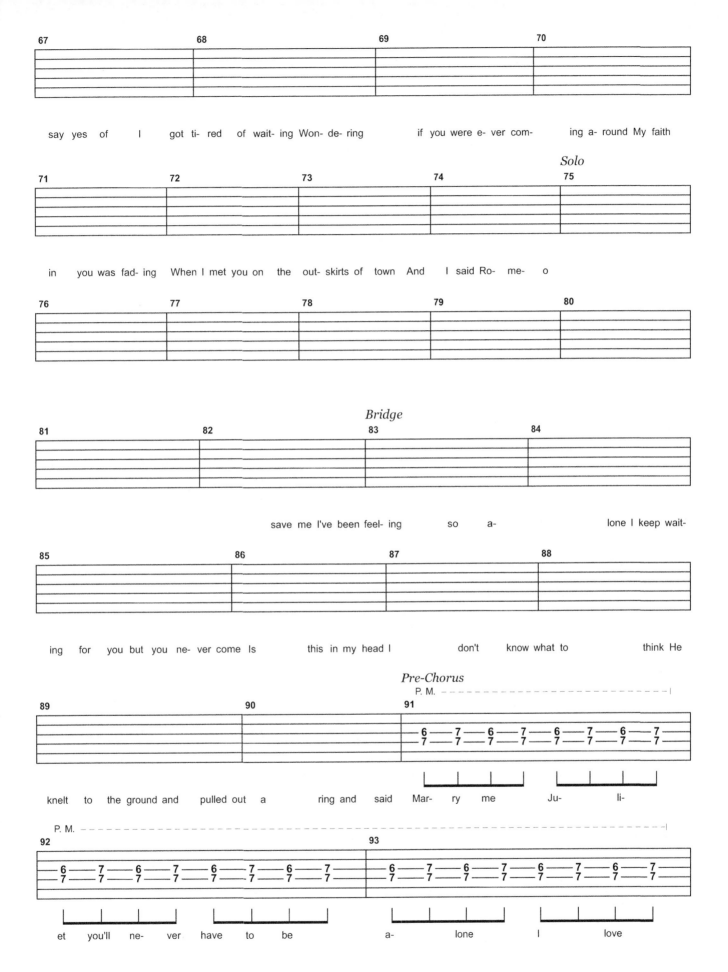

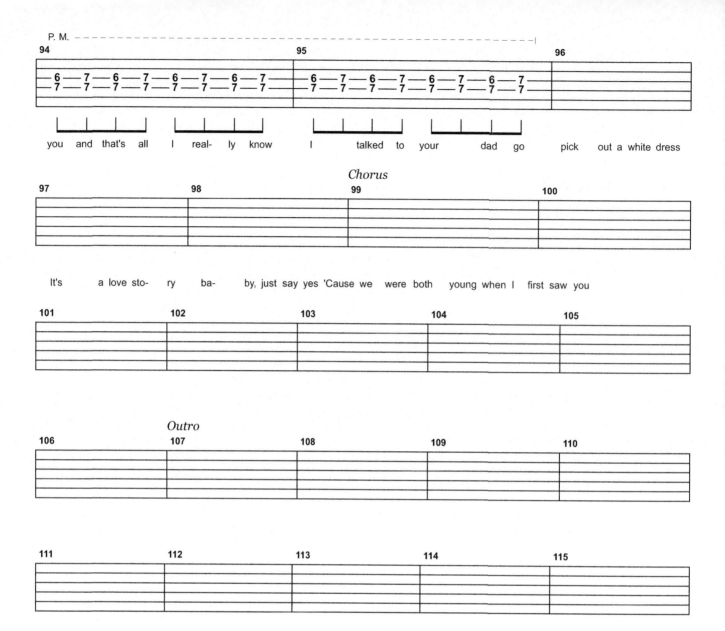

P. M. ---

```
94                                              95                                        96
|---6---7---6---7---6---7---6---7---|---6---7---6---7---6---7---6---7---|-------------------|
|---7---7---7---7---7---7---7---7---|---7---7---7---7---7---7---7---7---|-------------------|
|----------------------------------|----------------------------------|-------------------|
```

you and that's all   I   real- ly know   I   talked to your   dad go   pick   out a white dress

Chorus

```
97              98              99                100
|------------|------------|------------|------------|
|------------|------------|------------|------------|
|------------|------------|------------|------------|
|------------|------------|------------|------------|
|------------|------------|------------|------------|
|------------|------------|------------|------------|
```

It's   a love sto- ry   ba-   by, just say yes 'Cause we   were both   young when I first saw you

```
101             102             103             104             105
|------------|------------|------------|------------|------------|
|------------|------------|------------|------------|------------|
|------------|------------|------------|------------|------------|
|------------|------------|------------|------------|------------|
|------------|------------|------------|------------|------------|
|------------|------------|------------|------------|------------|
```

Outro

```
106             107             108             109             110
|------------|------------|------------|------------|------------|
|------------|------------|------------|------------|------------|
|------------|------------|------------|------------|------------|
|------------|------------|------------|------------|------------|
|------------|------------|------------|------------|------------|
|------------|------------|------------|------------|------------|
```

```
111             112             113             114             115
|------------|------------|------------|------------|------------|
|------------|------------|------------|------------|------------|
|------------|------------|------------|------------|------------|
|------------|------------|------------|------------|------------|
|------------|------------|------------|------------|------------|
|------------|------------|------------|------------|------------|
```

Taylor Swift - Love Story

Track: Mike Meadows II - Acoustic Guitar (Nylon)

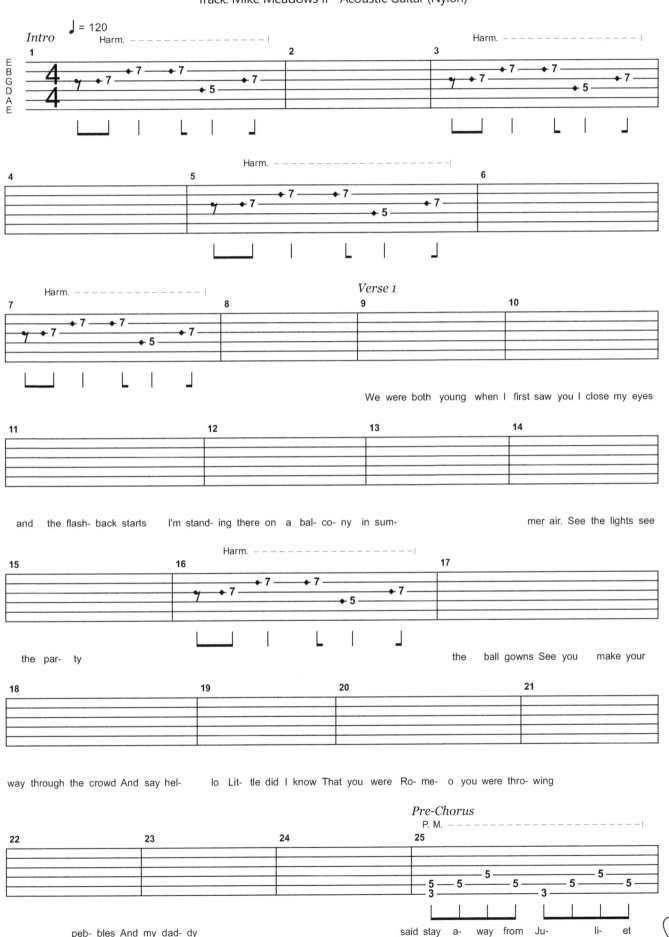

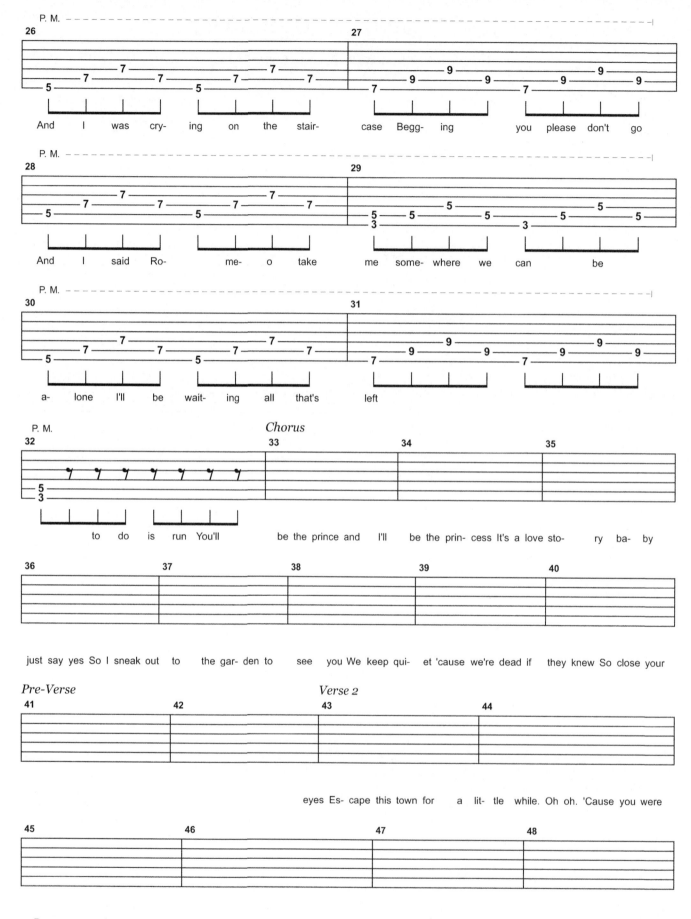

And I was cry- ing on the stair- case Begg- ing you please don't go

And I said Ro- me- o take me some- where we can be

a- lone I'll be wait- ing all that's left

Chorus

to do is run You'll be the prince and I'll be the prin- cess It's a love sto- ry ba- by

just say yes So I sneak out to the gar- den to see you We keep qui- et 'cause we're dead if they knew So close your

Pre-Verse   *Verse 2*

eyes Es- cape this town for a lit- tle while. Oh oh. 'Cause you were

Ro- me- o I was a scar- let let- ter And my dad- dy said stay a- way from Ju- li- et But

49 **50** **51** **52**

you were eve-   ry- thing   to   me, I was Begg- ing you please don't go And I said Ro- me- o take me some-

53 **54** **55** **56**

where we can   be a- lone I'll be wait- ing all   that's left to do is run You'll be   the prince and I'll be the prin- cess It's a

Chorus

57 **58** **59** **60**

love   sto- ry ba- by just   say yes Ro-   me-   o   save me they're trying to tell me

61 **62** **63** **64** **65**

how   to feel This love is dif- fi- cult but it's real Don't be a- fraid we'll make it out   of   this mess It's a   love

66 **67** **68** **69**

sto- ry ba-   by   just   say yes of   I   got ti- red of wait- ing Won- de- ring   if you were e- ver com-

70 **71** **72** **73** **74**

ing a- round My faith in   you was fad- ing When I met you on the out- skirts of town And   I said Ro- me- o

Solo

75 **76** **77** **78** **79**

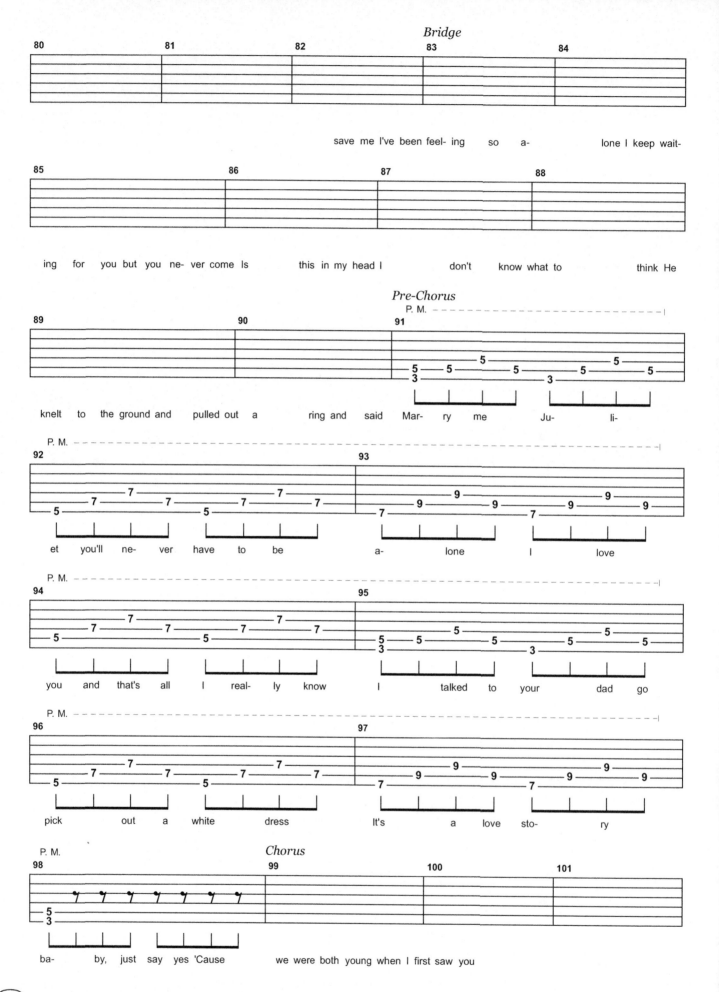

102 **103** **104** **105** **106**

Outro

107 **108** **109** **110** **111**

112 **113** **114** **115**

Taylor Swift
Better Than Revenge

Taylor Swift - Better Than Revenge

Track: Acoustic - Acoustic Guitar (Steel)

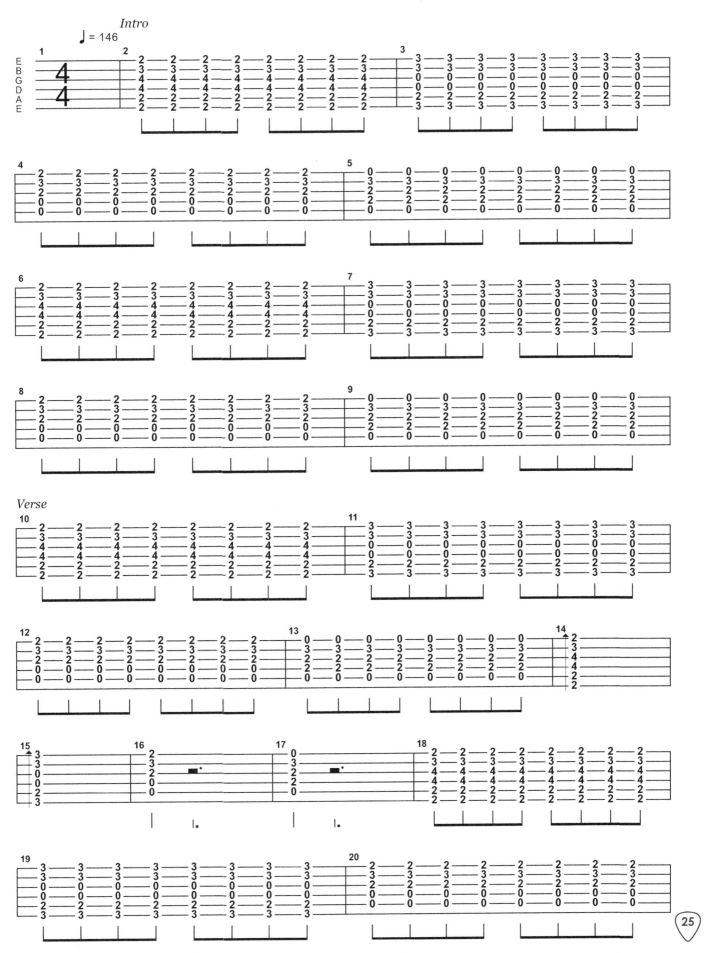

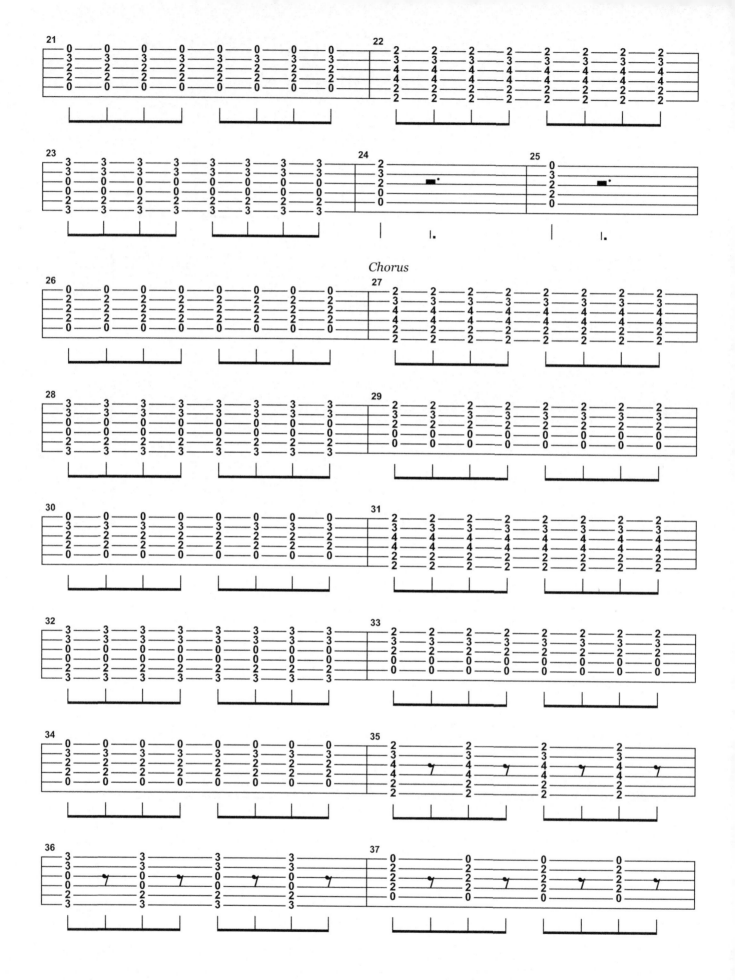

Chorus

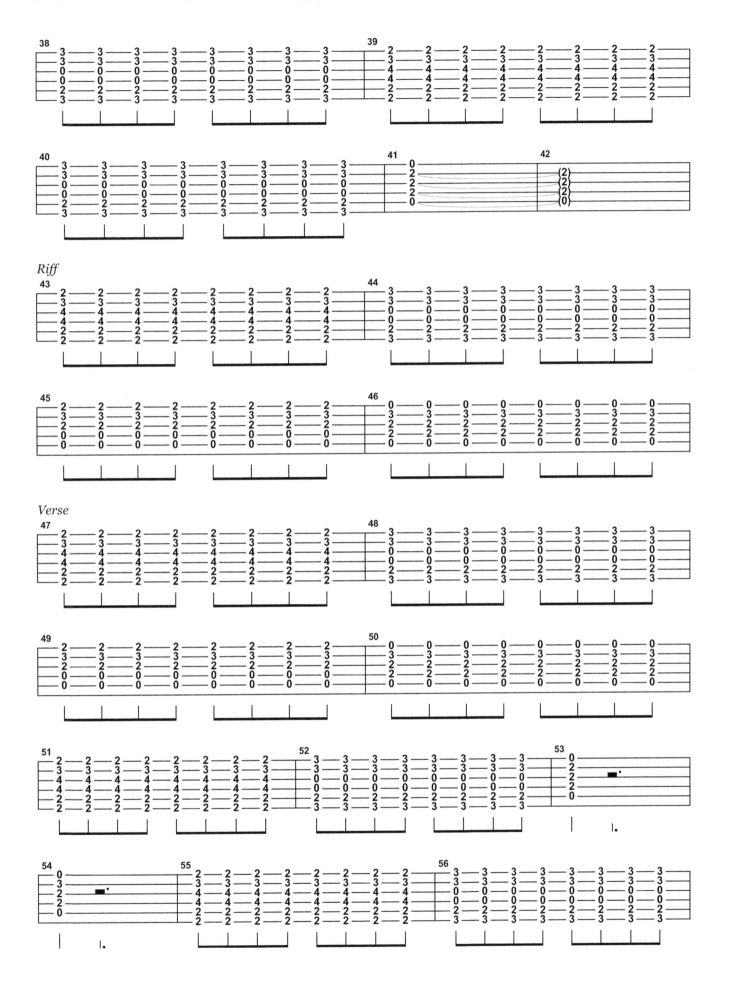

Riff

Verse

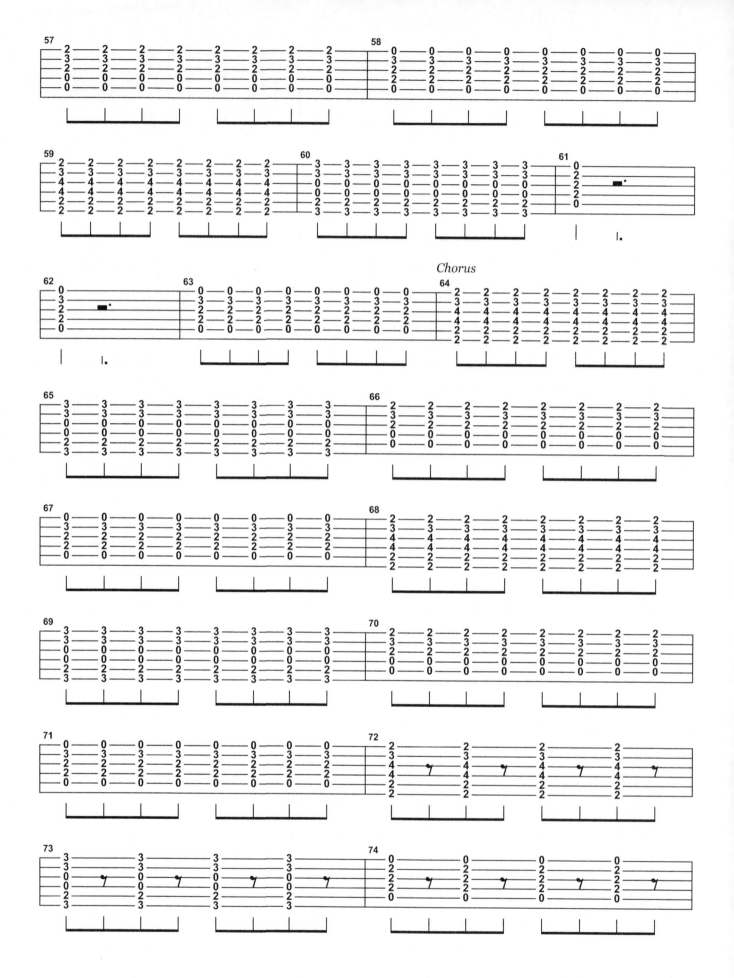

Chorus

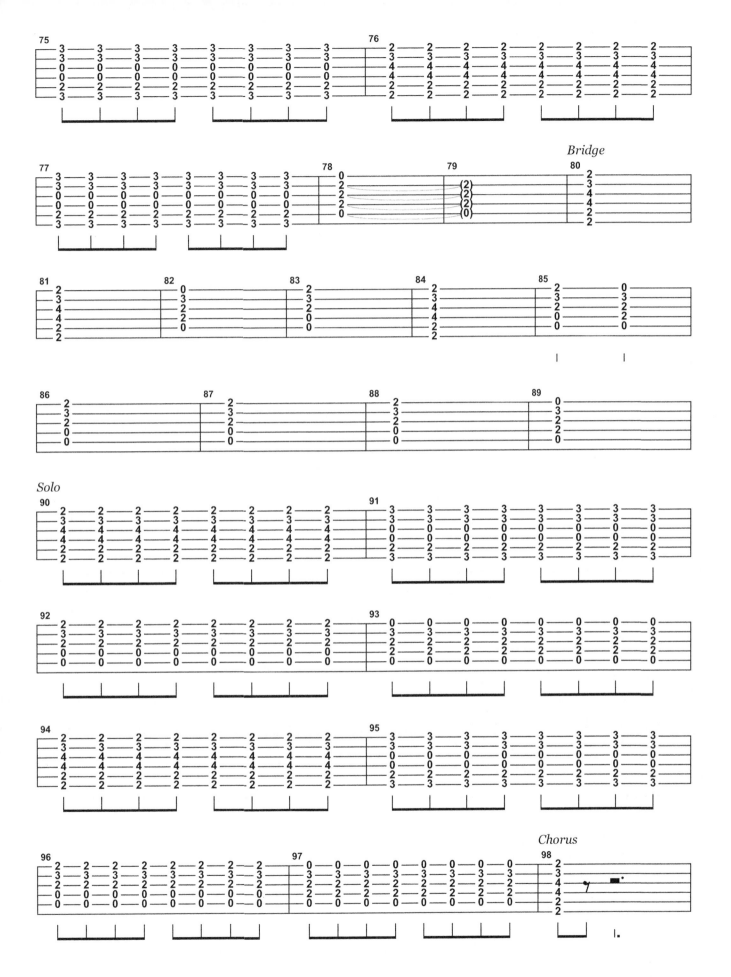

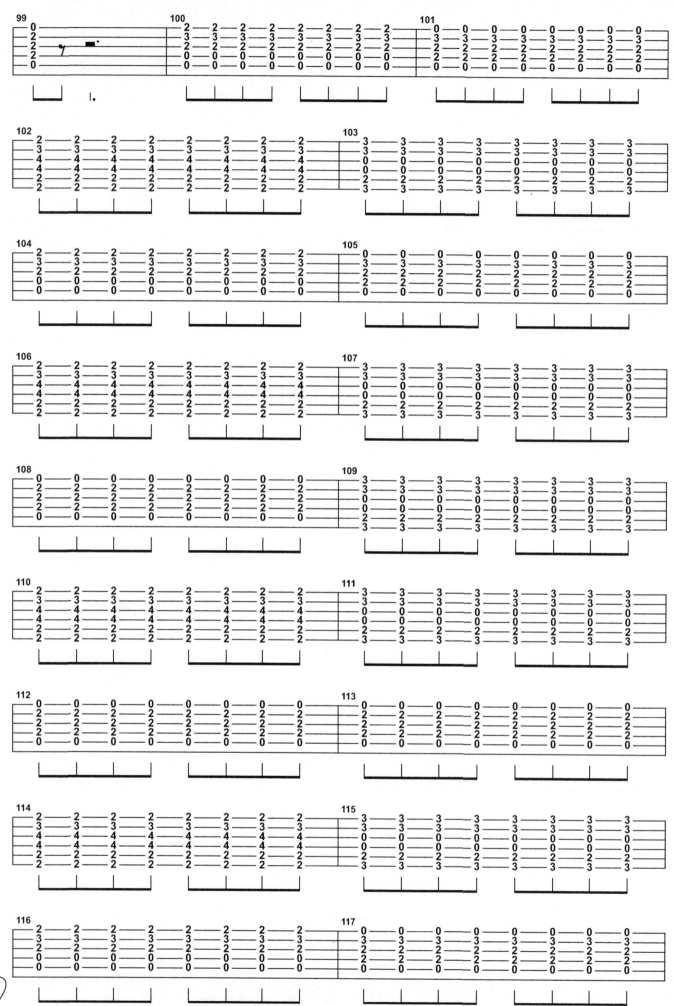

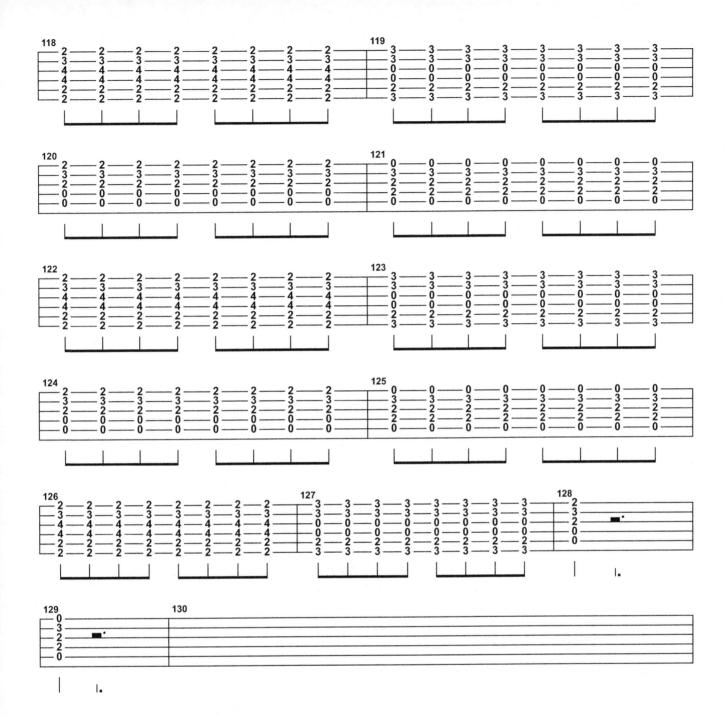

Taylor Swift

You Belong With Me

Taylor Swift - You Belong With Me

Track: Acoustic Guitar - Acoustic Guitar (Nylon)

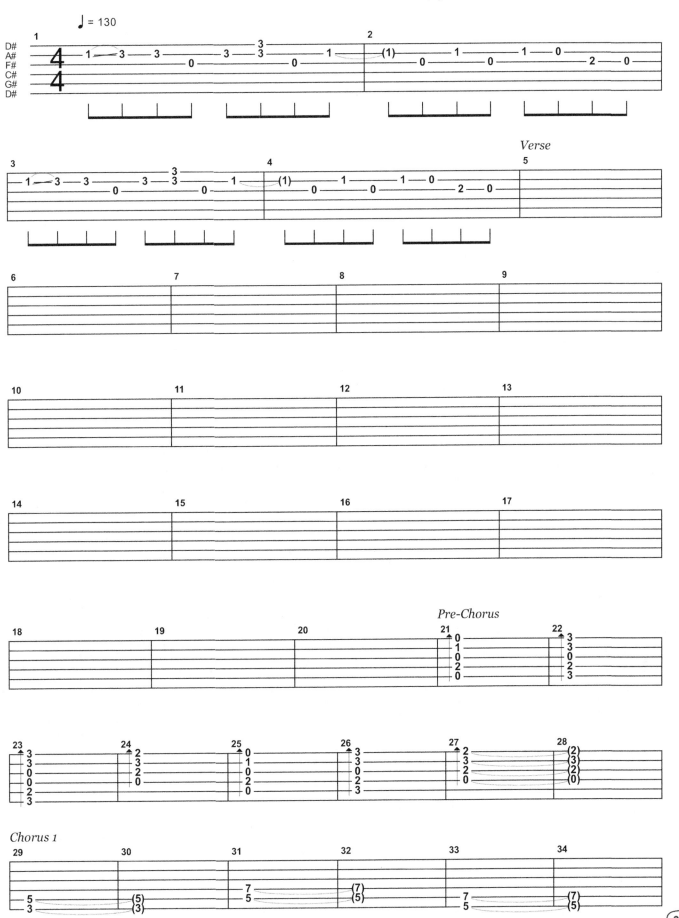

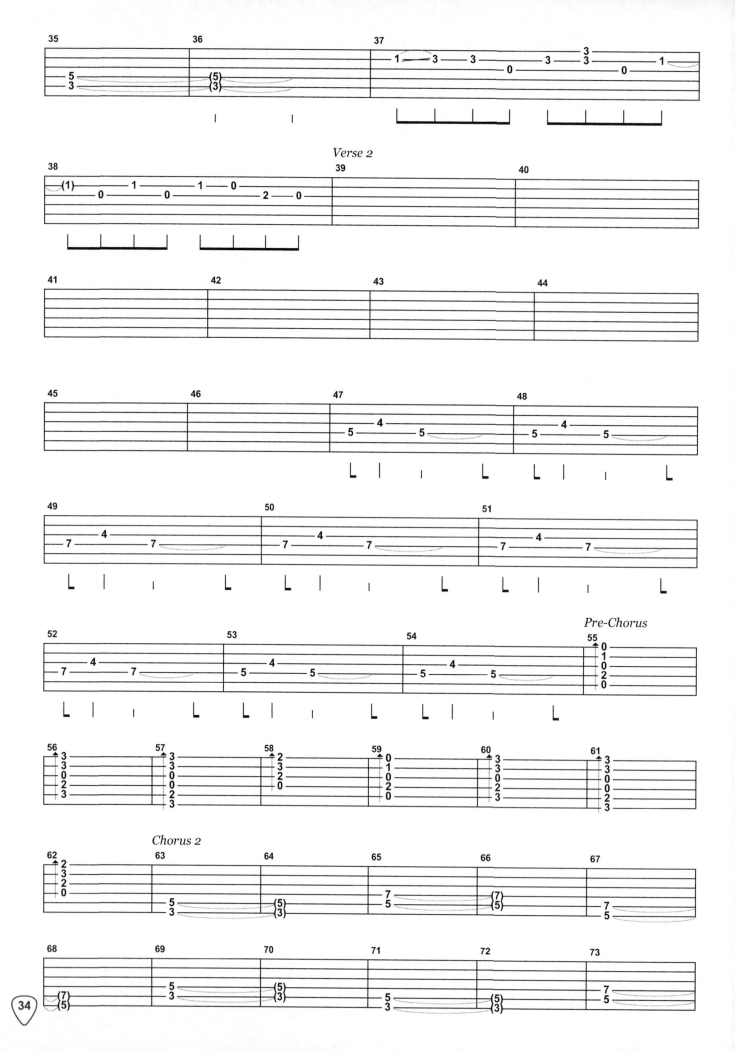

Verse 2

Pre-Chorus

Chorus 2

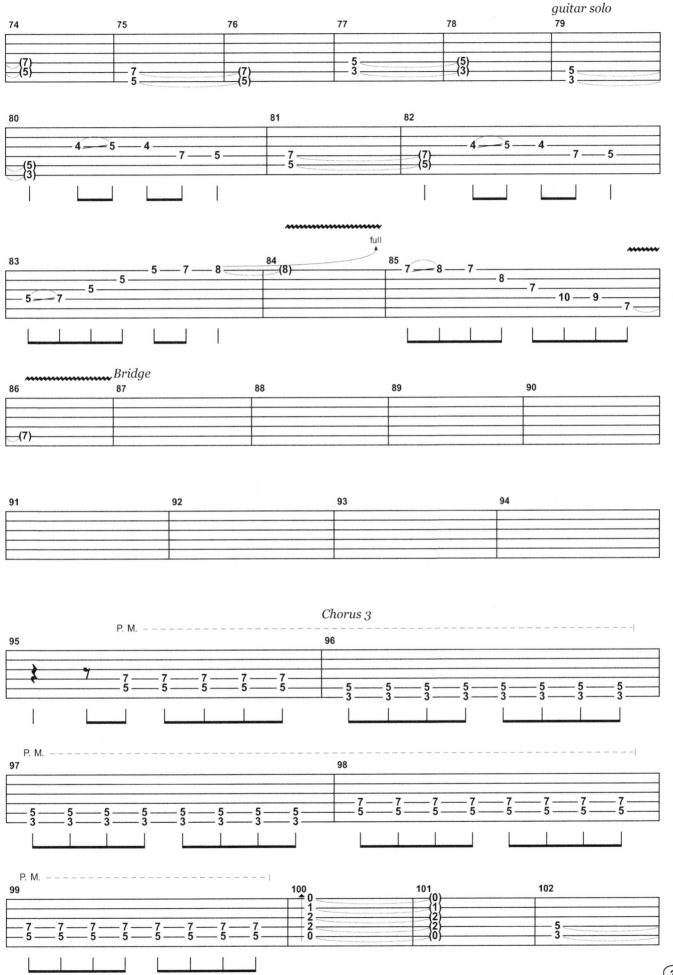

Ending

Taylor Swift
Safe And Sound

Taylor Swift - Safe And Sound

Track: Track 1 - Acoustic Guitar (Steel)

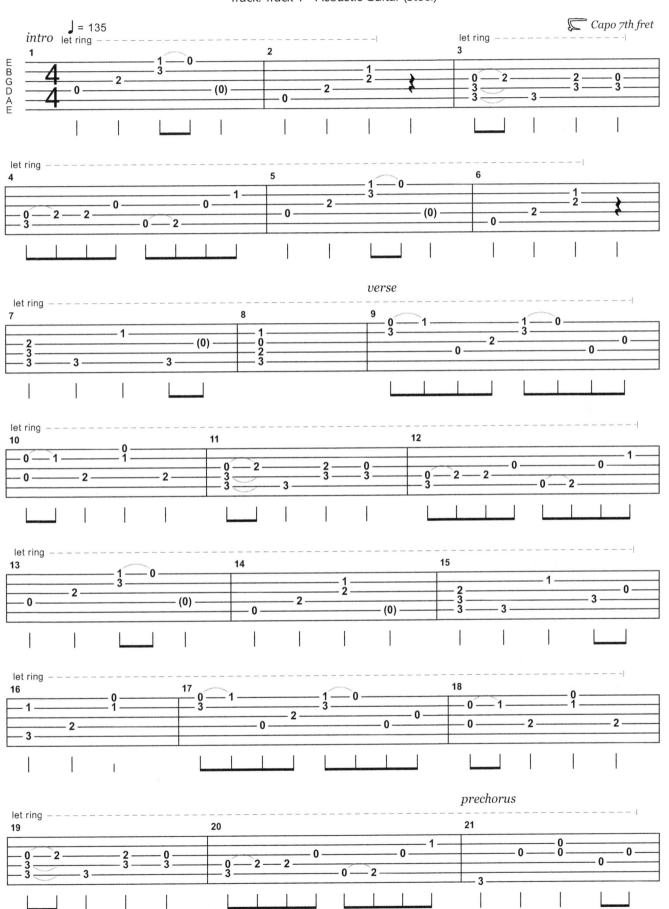

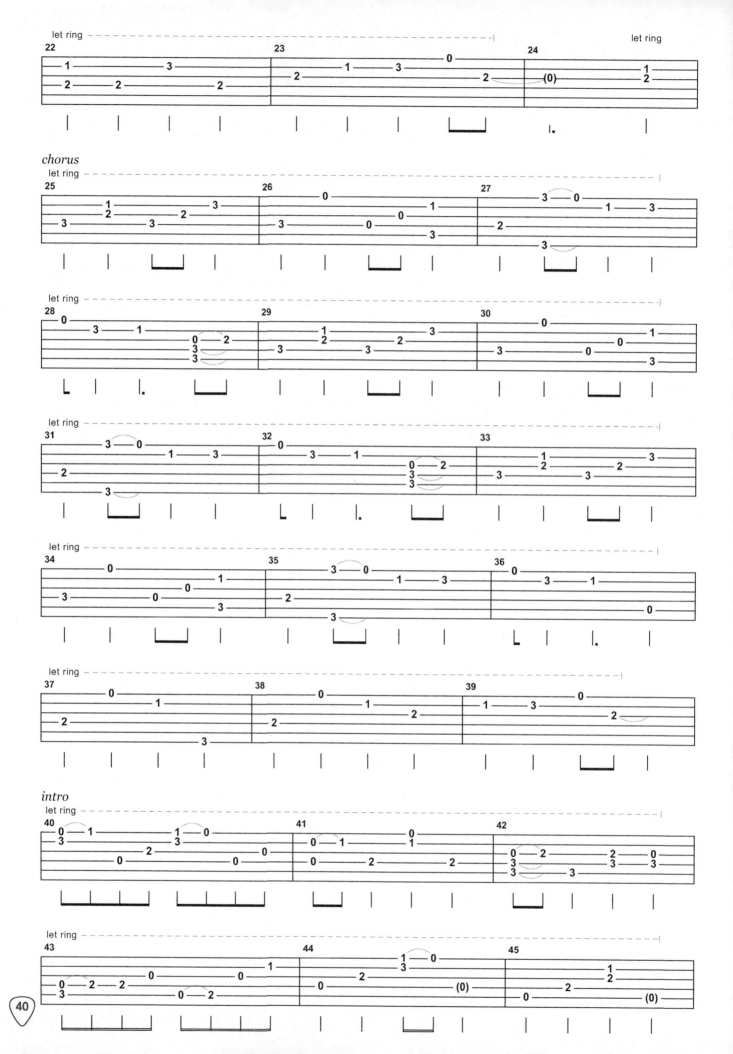

chorus

intro

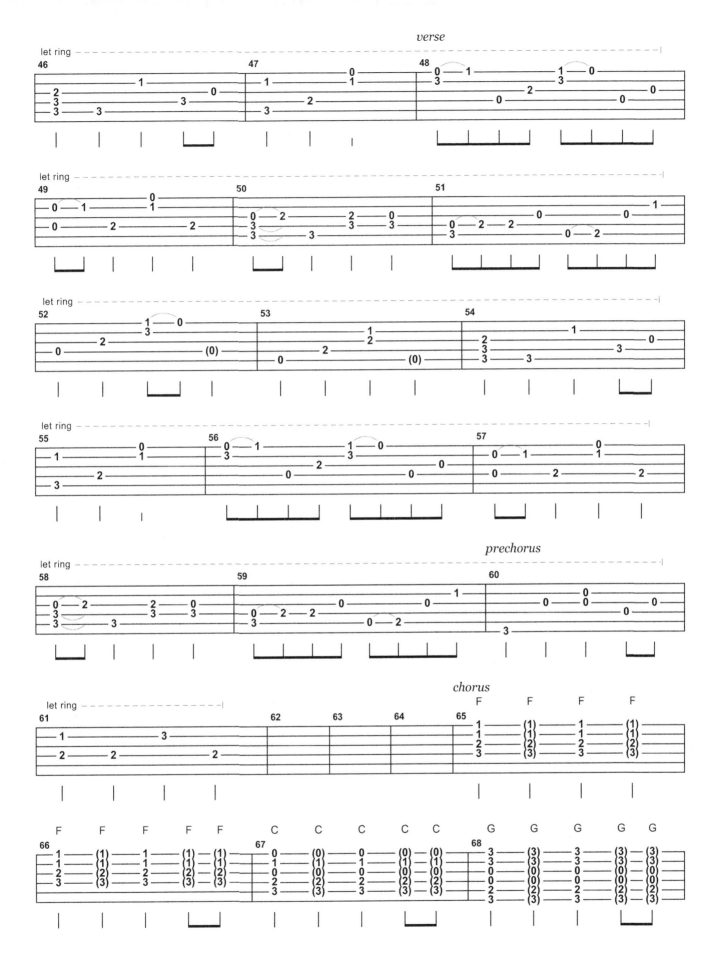

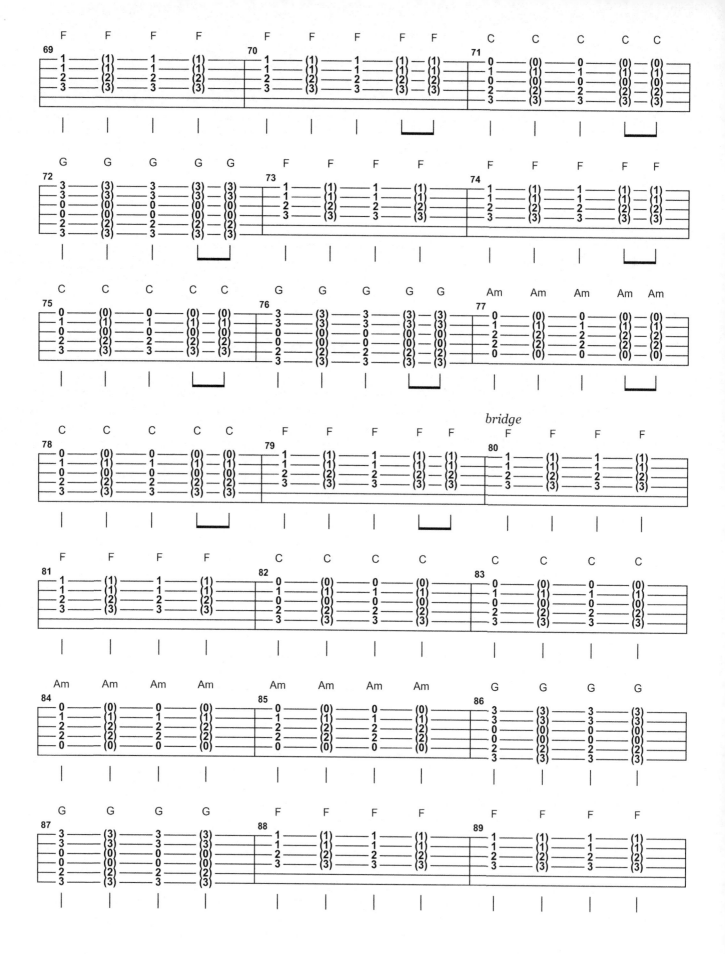

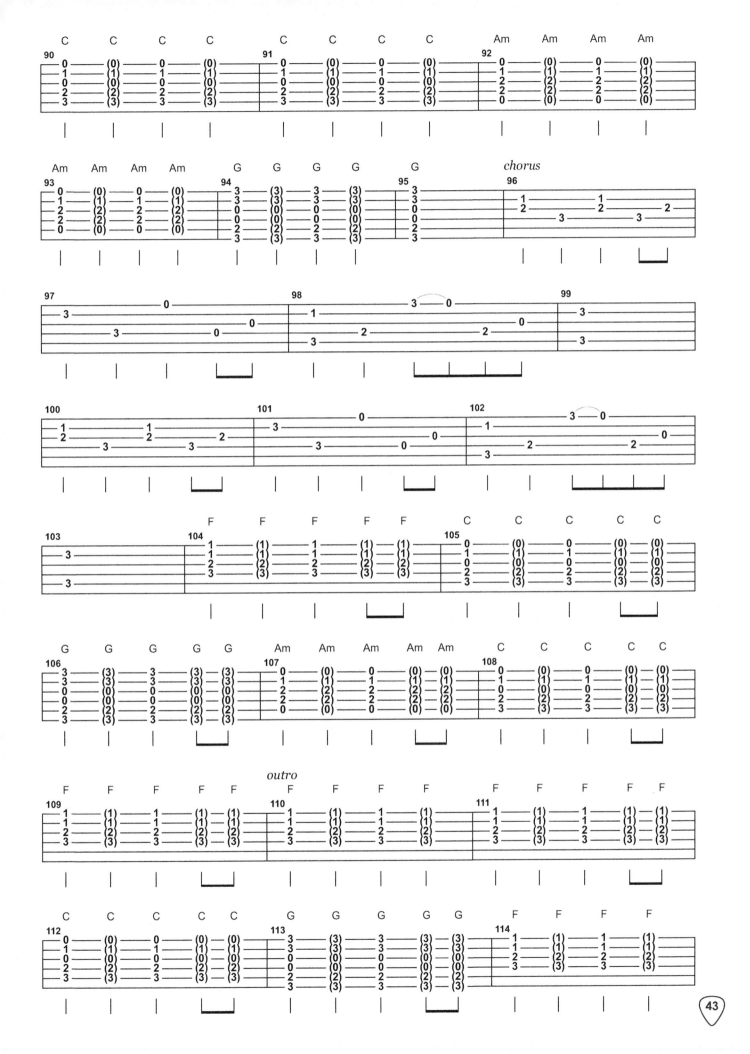

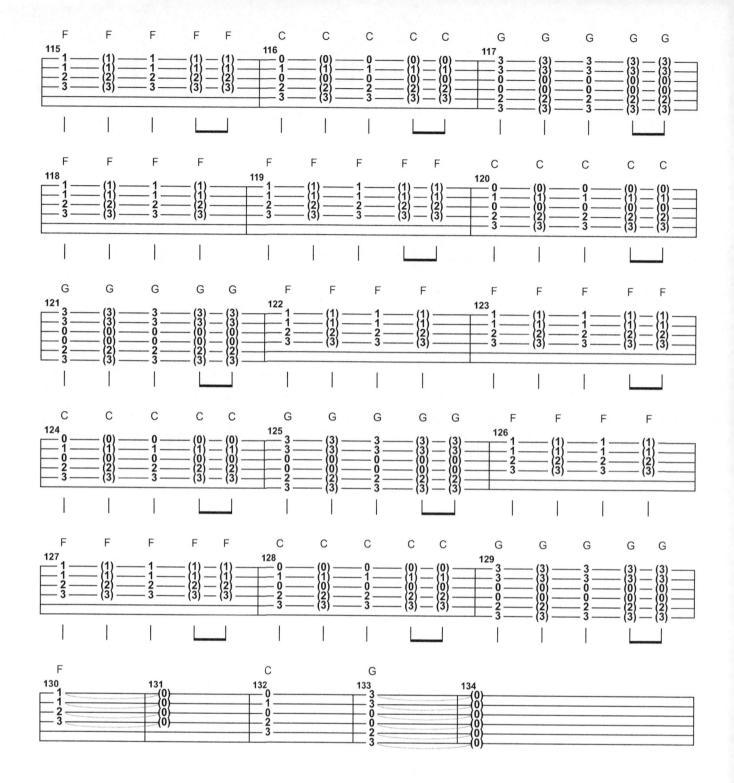

Taylor Swift
Fearless

Taylor Swift - Fearless

Track: Track 7 - Acoustic Guitar (Steel)

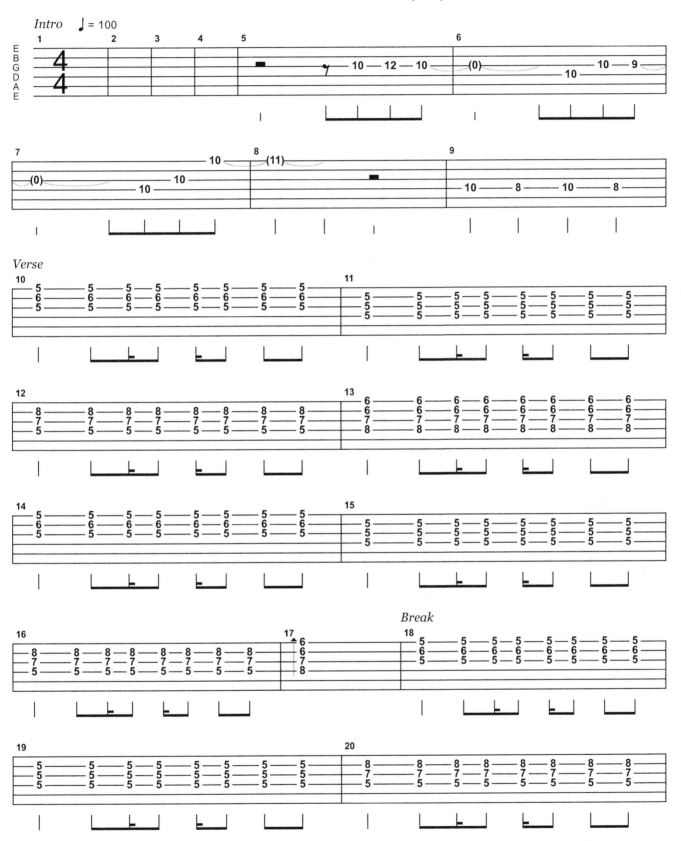

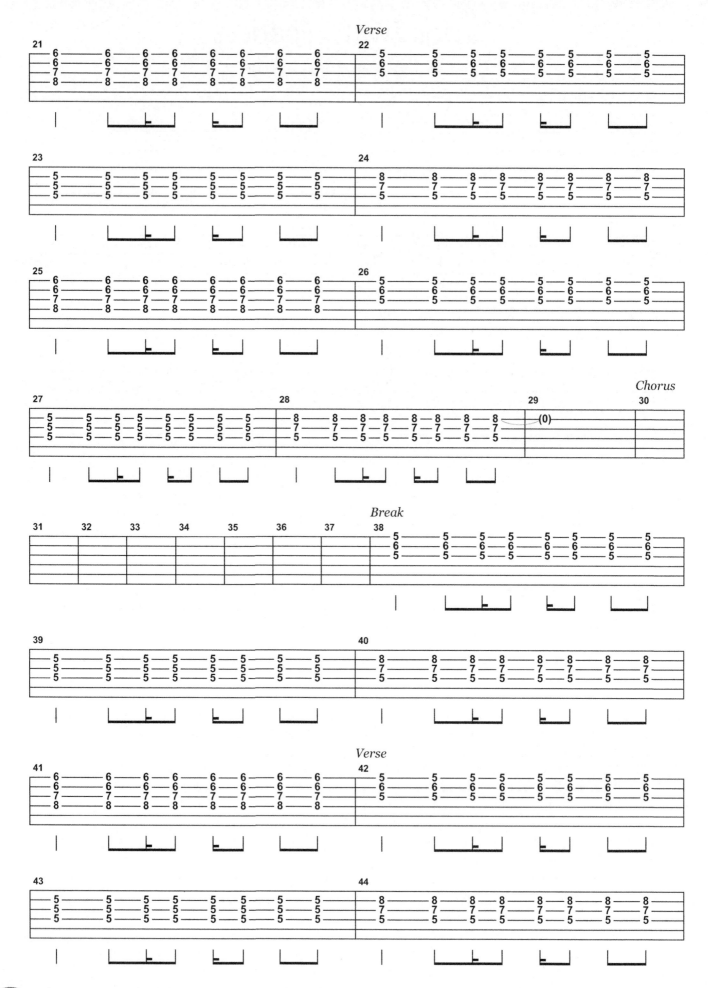

48

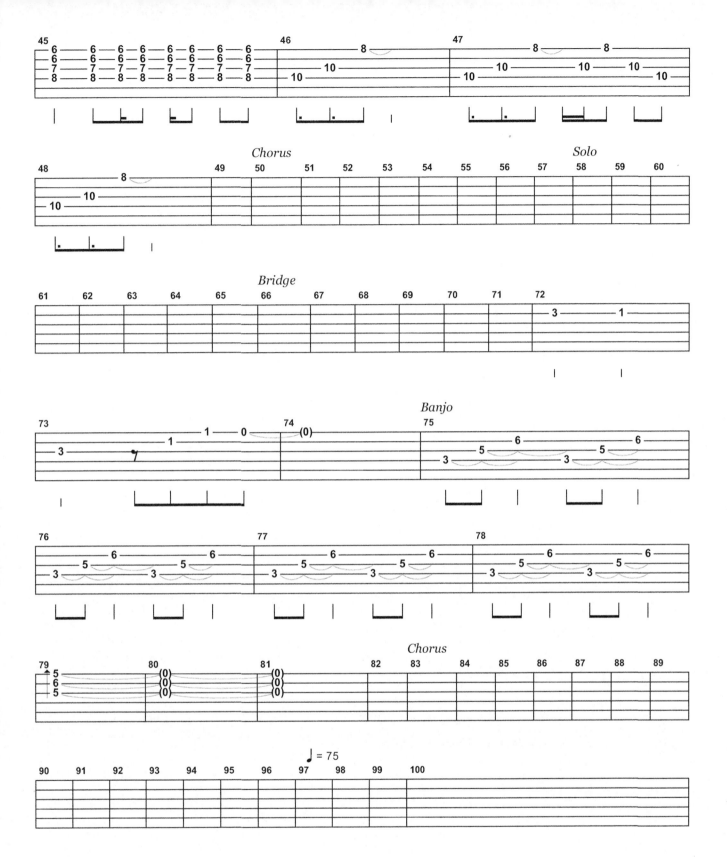

Taylor Swift

Back To December

Taylor Swift - Back To December

Track: Guitar 1 - Acoustic Guitar (Steel)

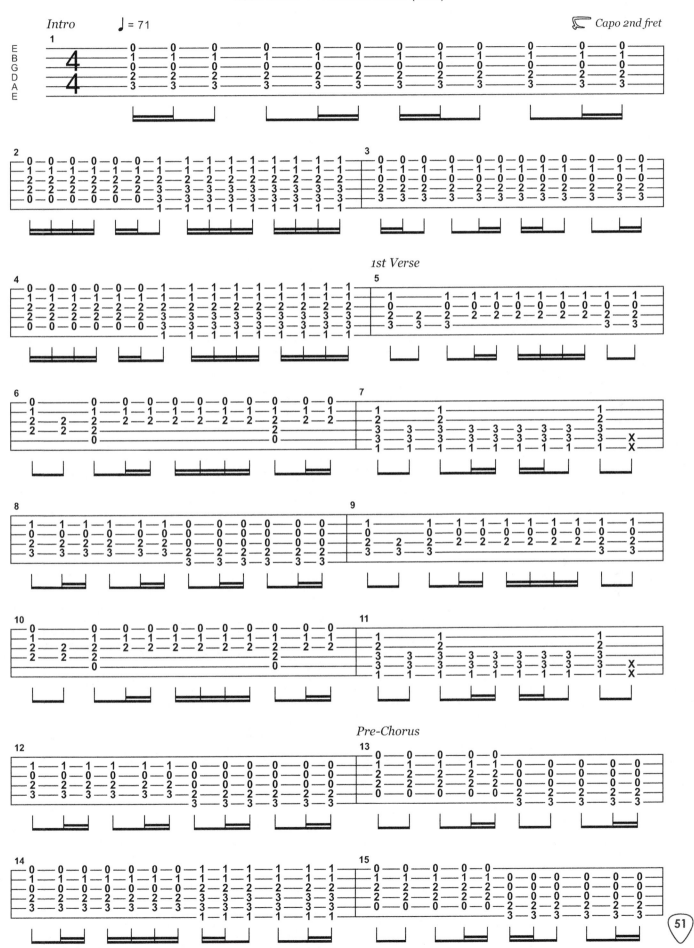

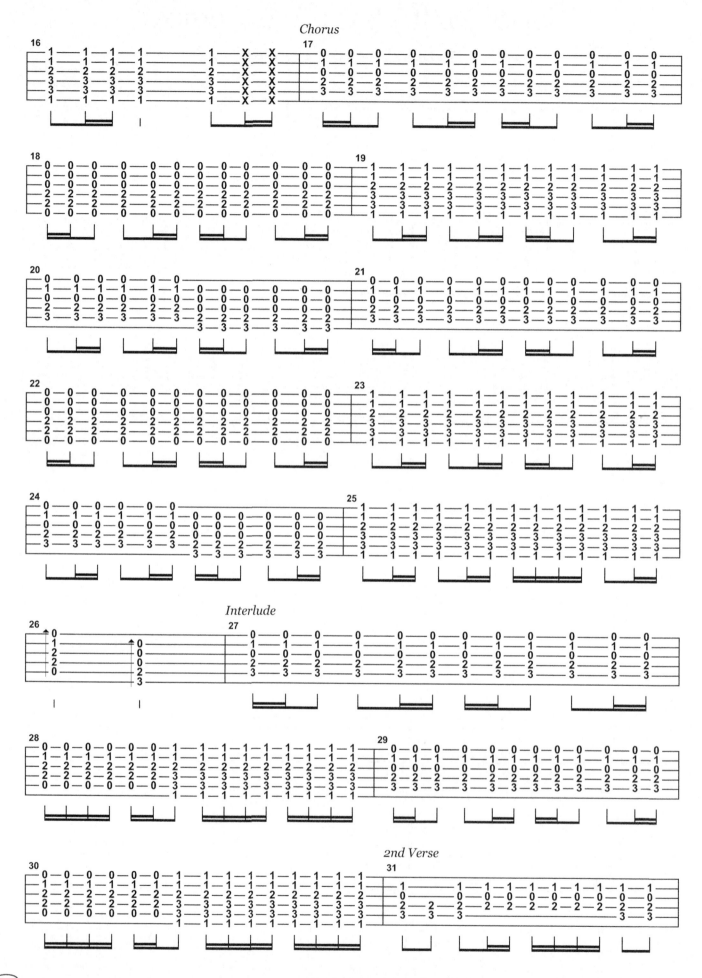

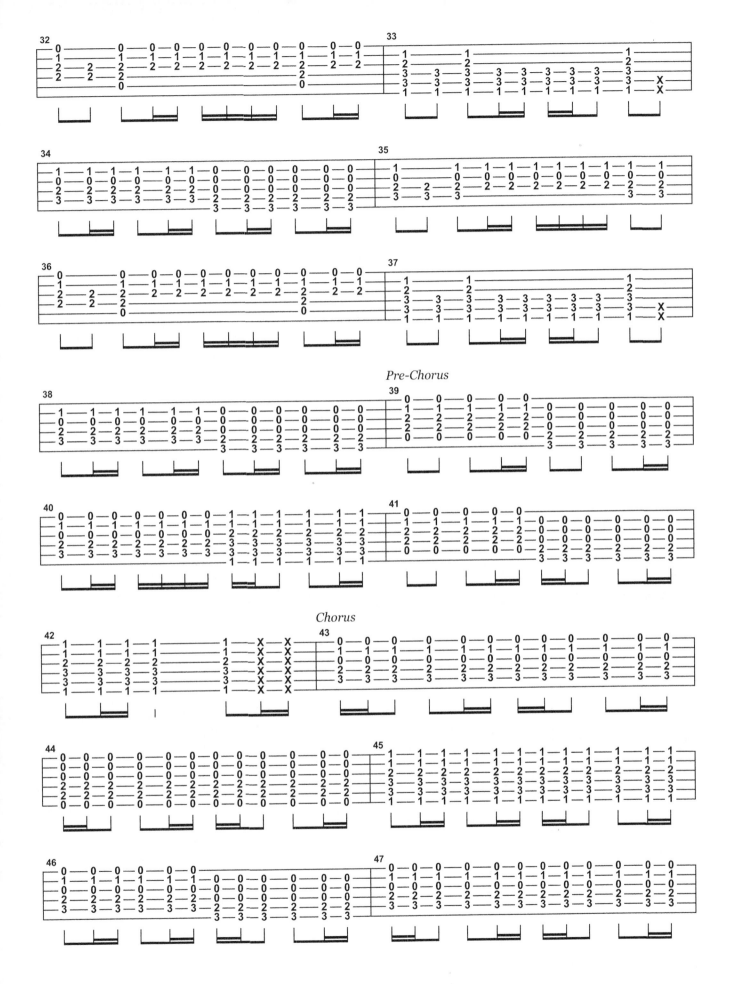

Pre-Chorus

Chorus

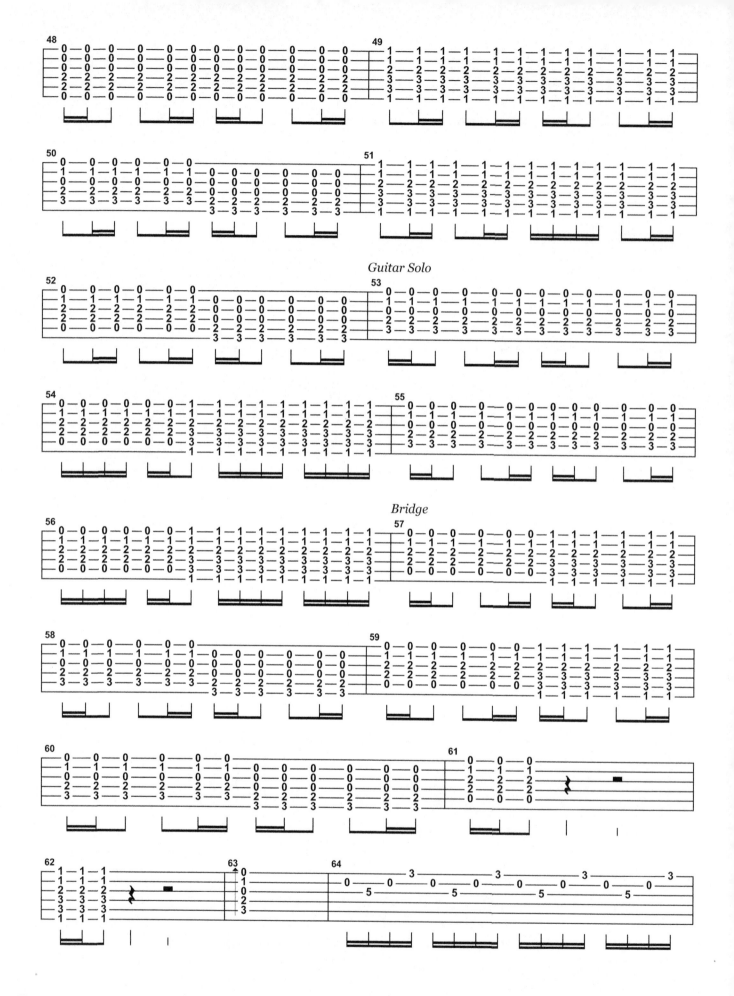

Guitar Solo

Bridge

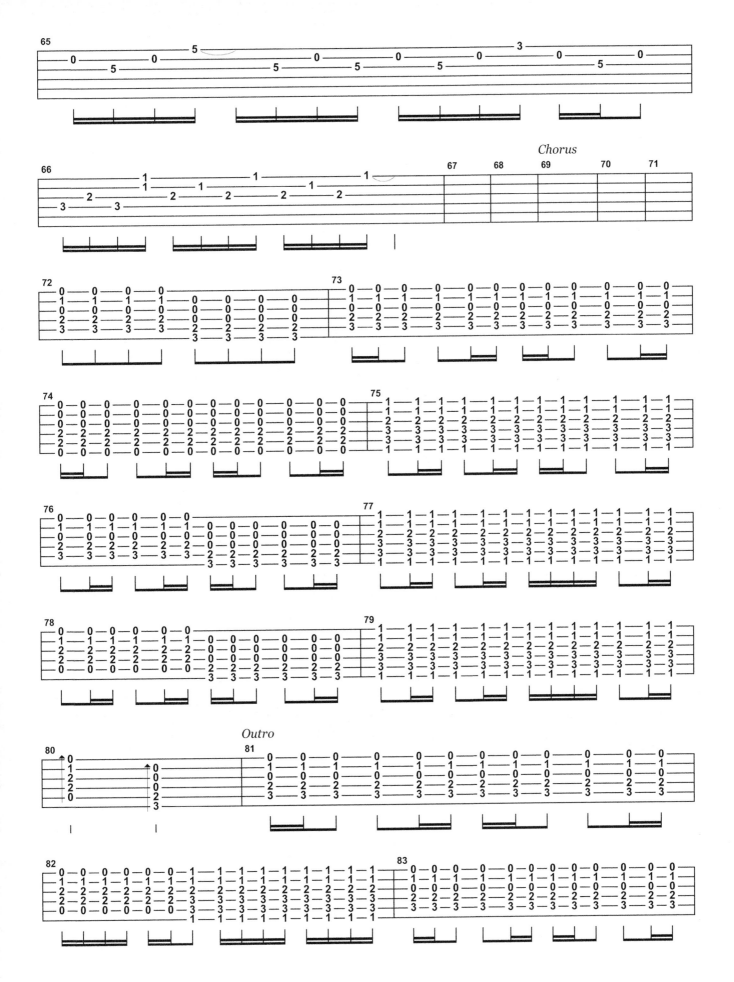

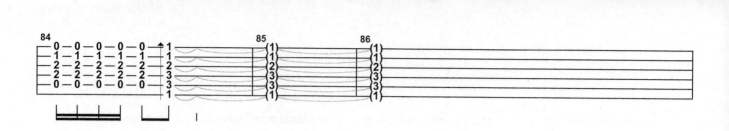

Taylor Swift - Back To December

Track: Guitar 2 - Acoustic Guitar (Steel)

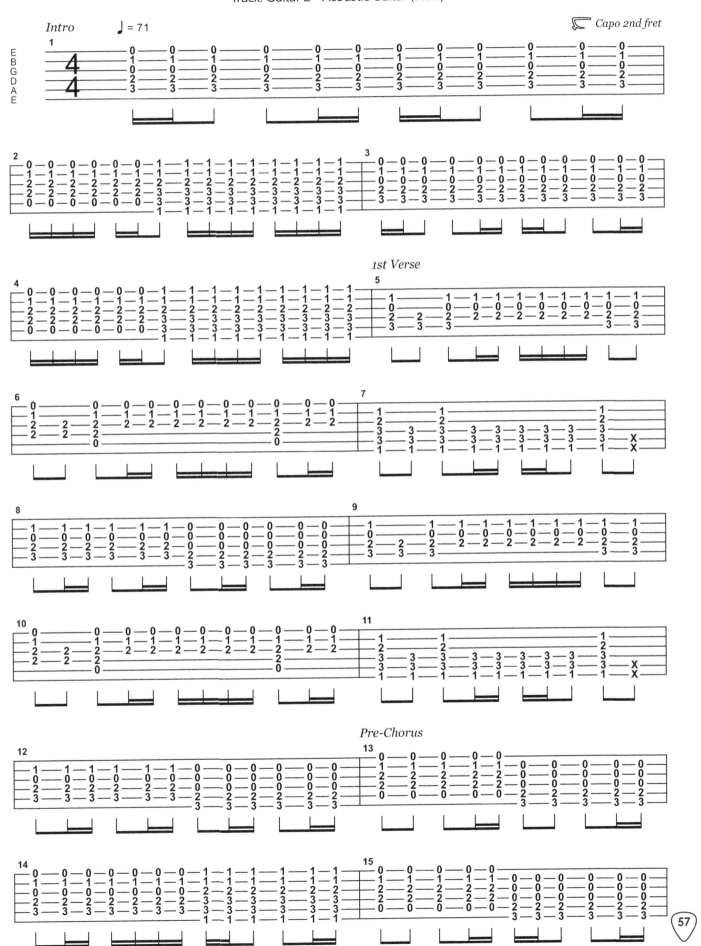

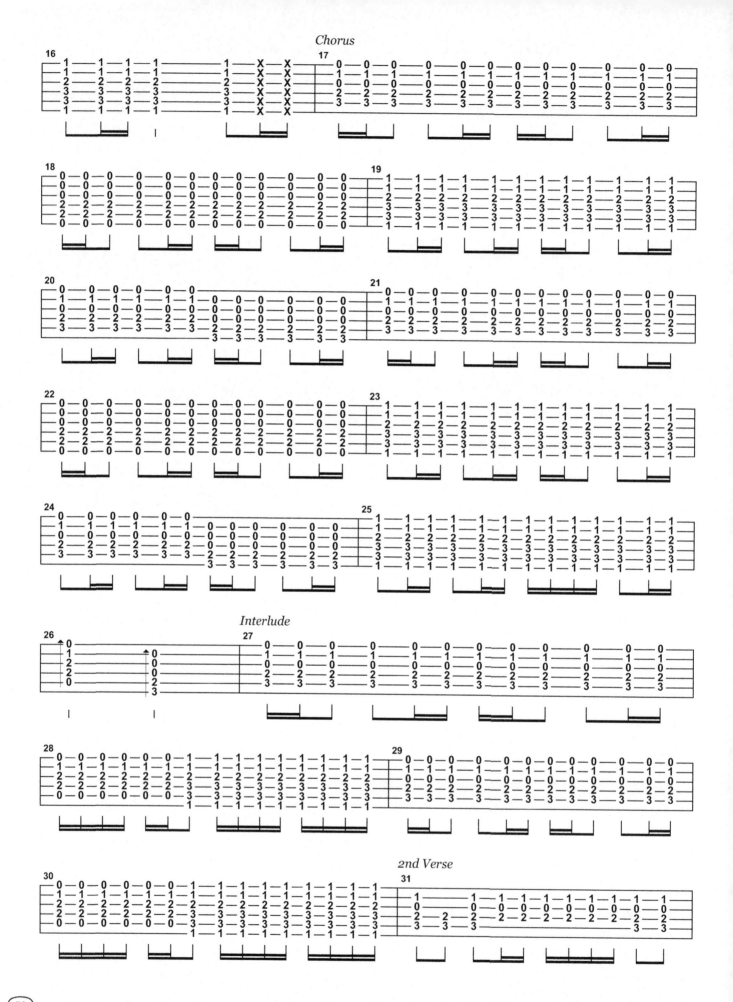

Chorus

Interlude

2nd Verse

58

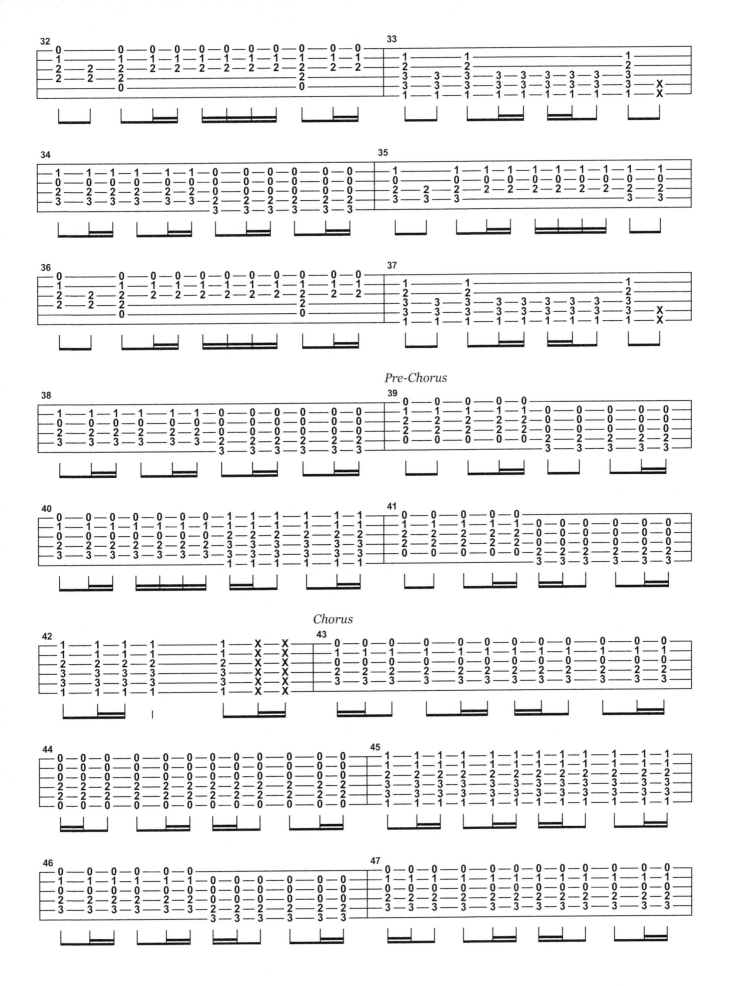

Pre-Chorus

Chorus

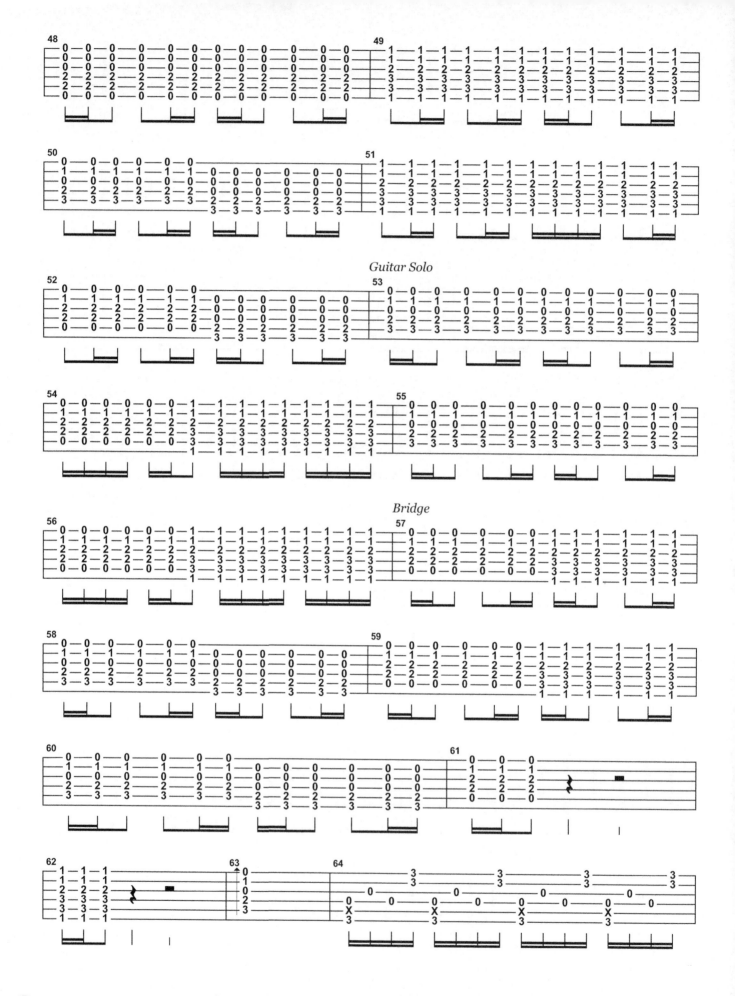

Guitar Solo

Bridge

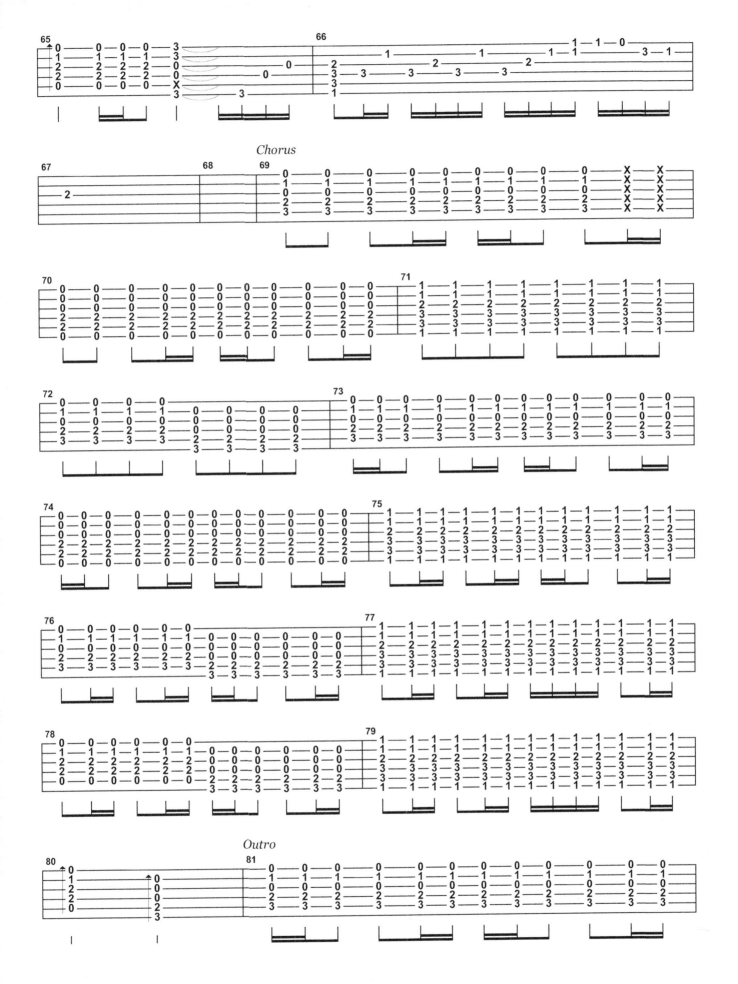

Chorus

Outro

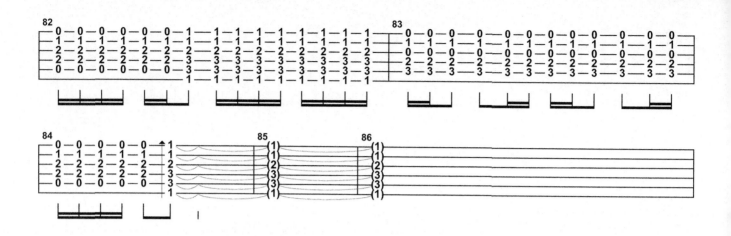

Taylor Swift - Back To December

Track: Guitar 3 - Acoustic Guitar (Steel)

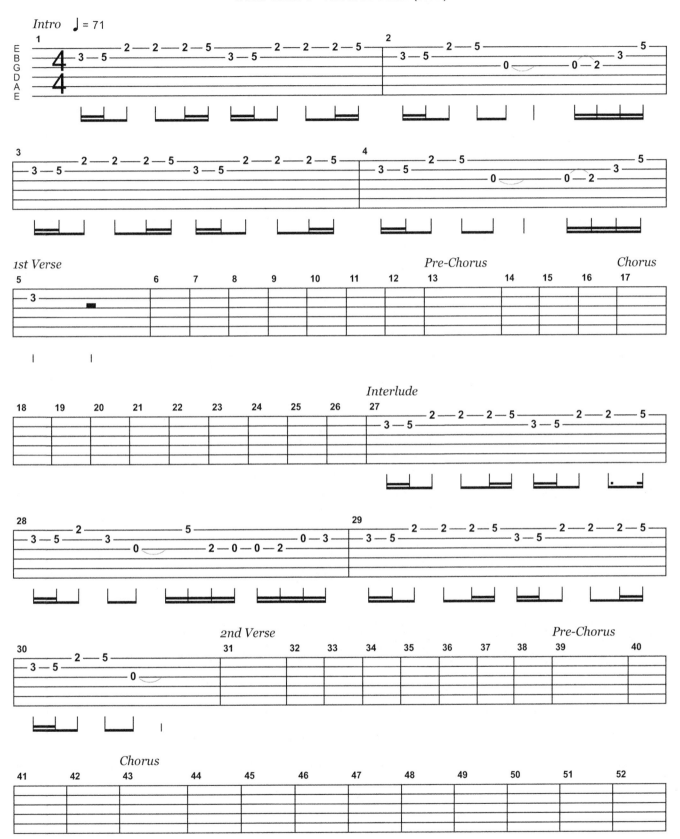

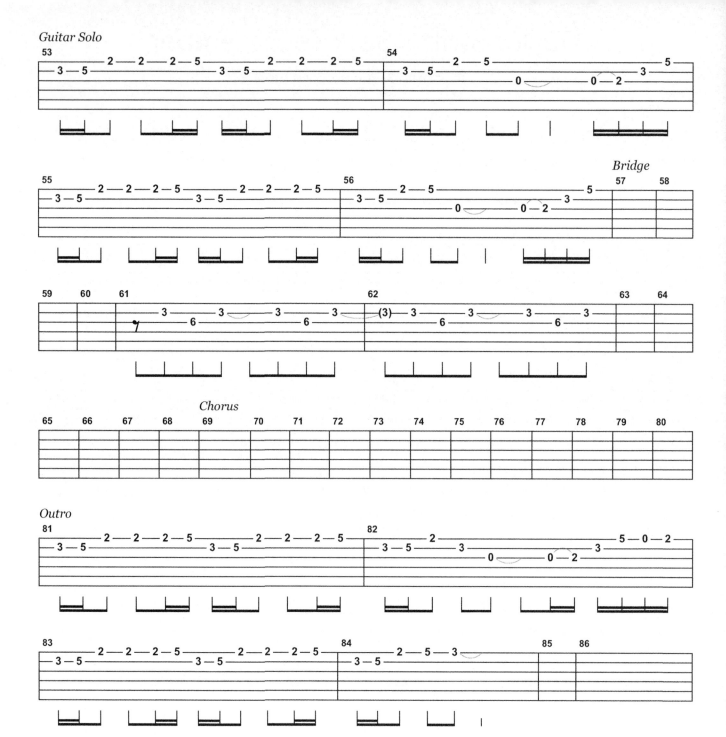

64

Taylor Swift

I knew You Were Trouble

Taylor Swift - I Knew You Were Trouble
(Full Band)

Track: Acoustic - Acoustic Guitar (Nylon)

♩ = 154   However, I've added a few bits of guitar myself.
Note: Everything in the song is in this tab.

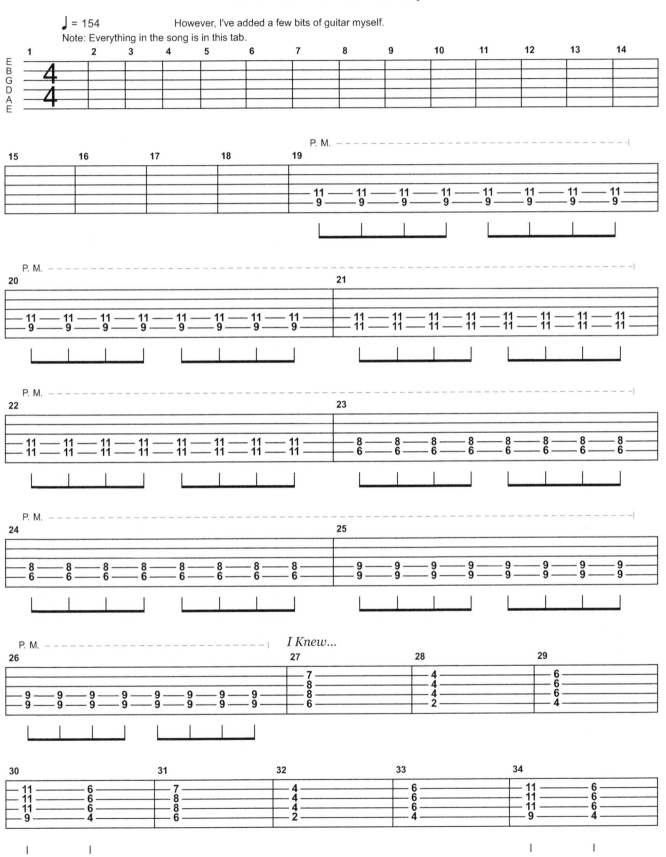

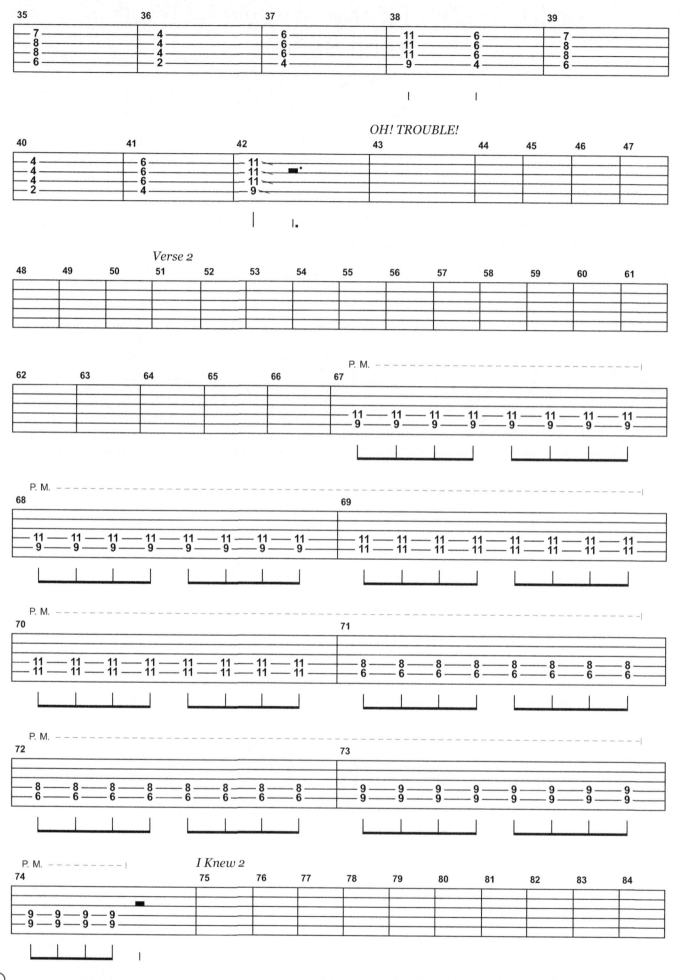

OH! TROUBLE!

Verse 2

I Knew 2

OH!! TROUBLE!!

85	86	87	88	89	90	91	92	93	94	95	96	97

The Saddest...   *I Knew 3*

98	99	100	101	102	103	104	105	106	107	108	109	110

111	112	113	114	115	116	117	118	119	120	121	122	123

OH!!! TROUBLE!!!   *I Knew 4*

124	125	126	127	128	129	130	131	132	133	134	135

136	137	138	139

Taylor Swift – I Knew You Were Trouble
(Full Band)

Track: Light Distortion - Acoustic Guitar (Steel)

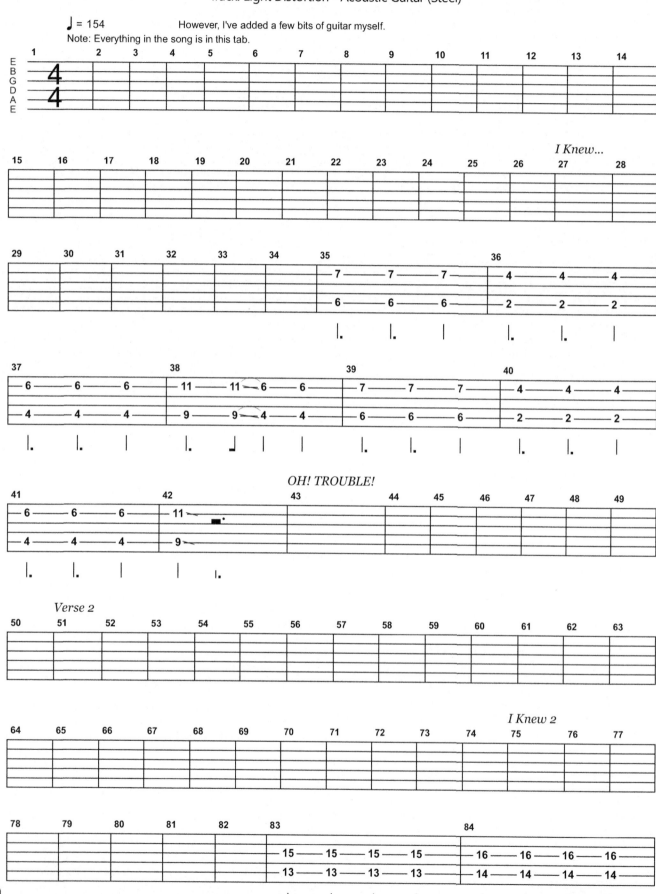

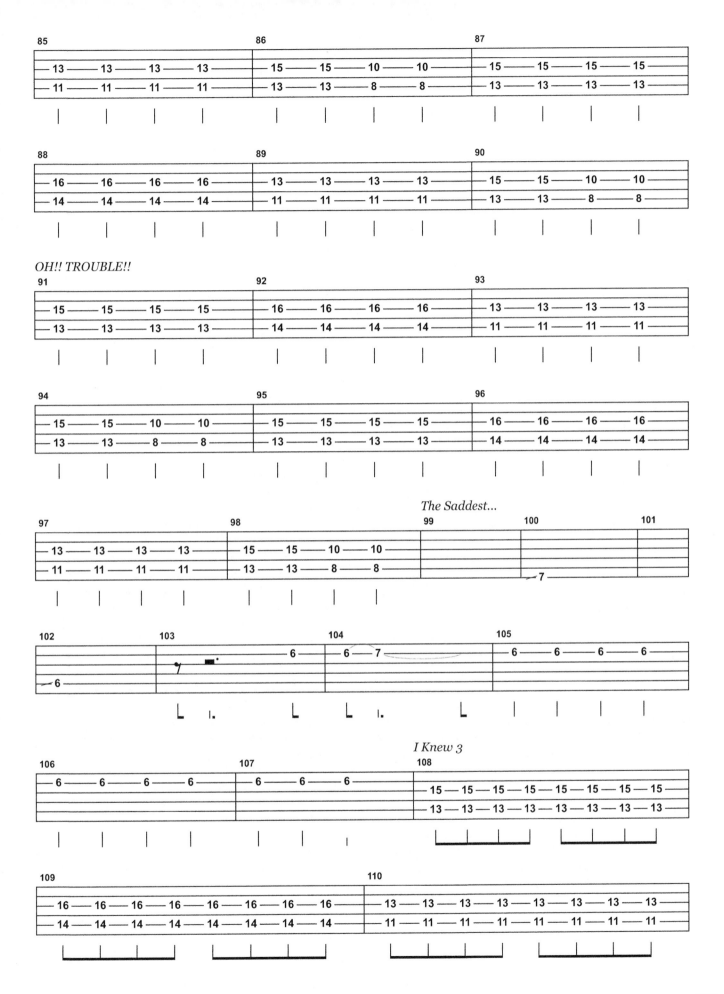

OH!! TROUBLE!!

The Saddest...

I Knew 3

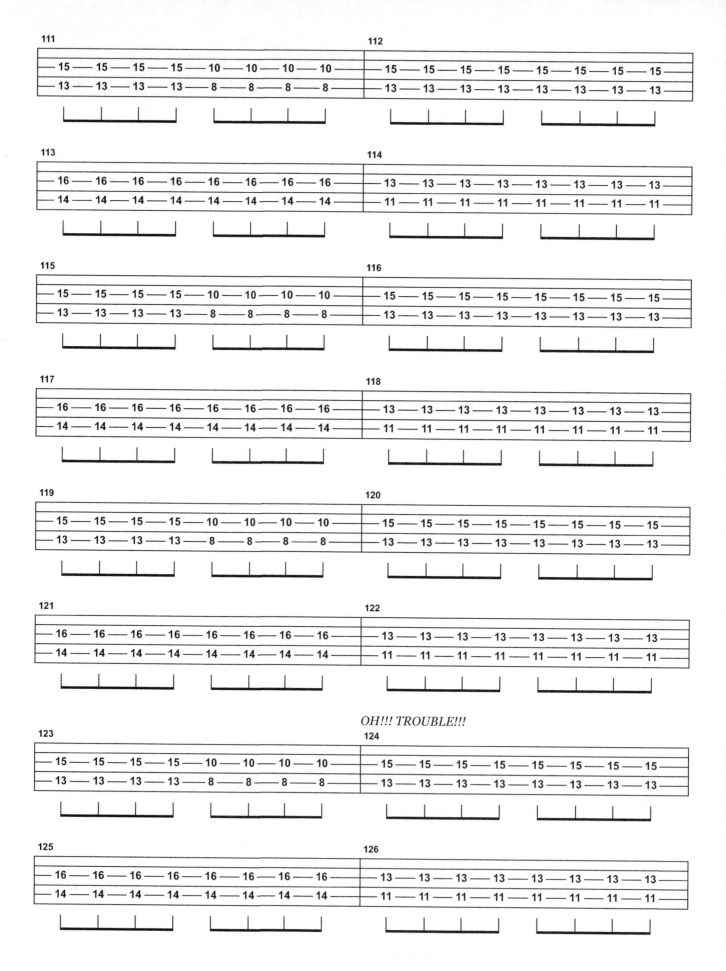

OH!!! TROUBLE!!!

I Knew 4

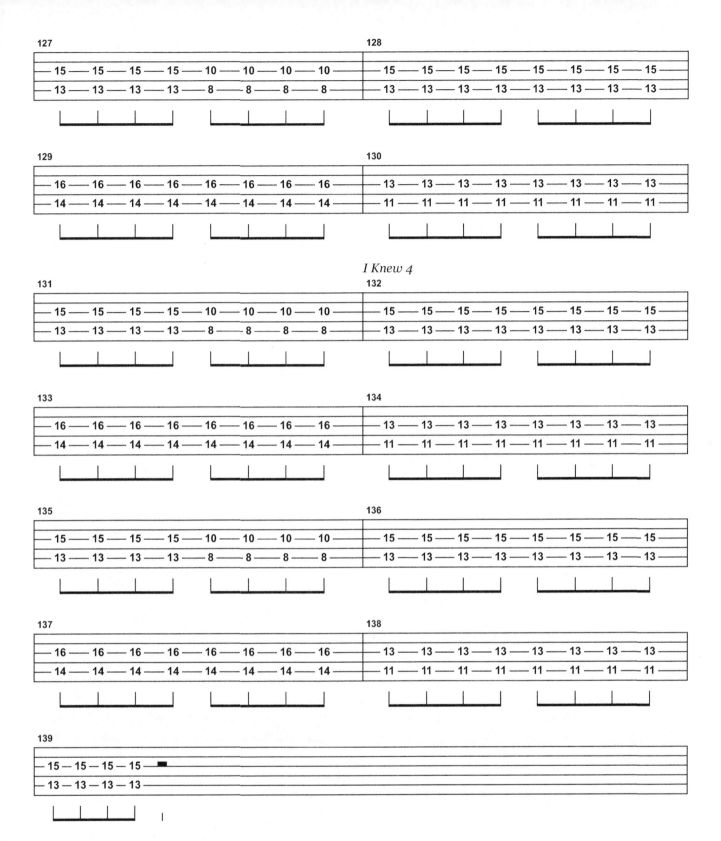

Taylor Swift

We Are Never Getting Back Together

Taylor Swift - We Are Never Getting Back Together

Track: Guitar - Acoustic Guitar (Steel)

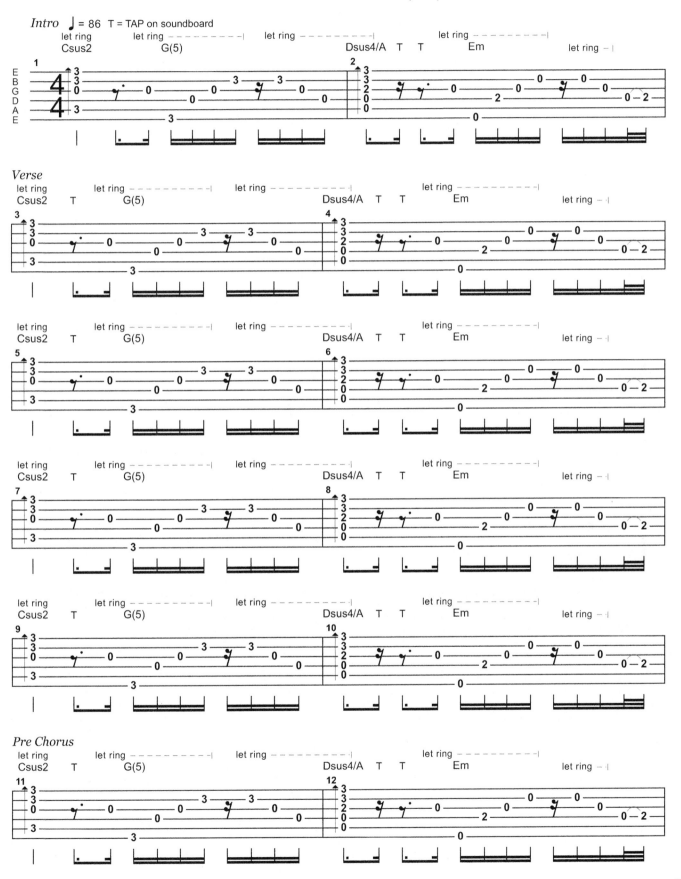

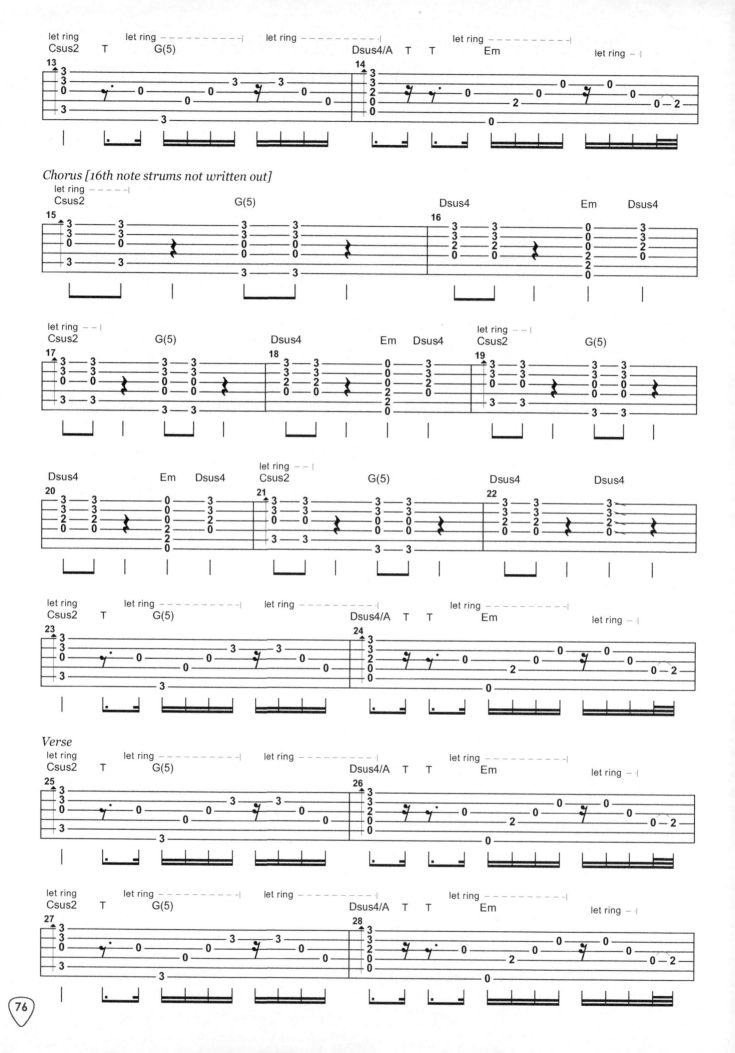

Chorus [16th note strums not written out]

Verse

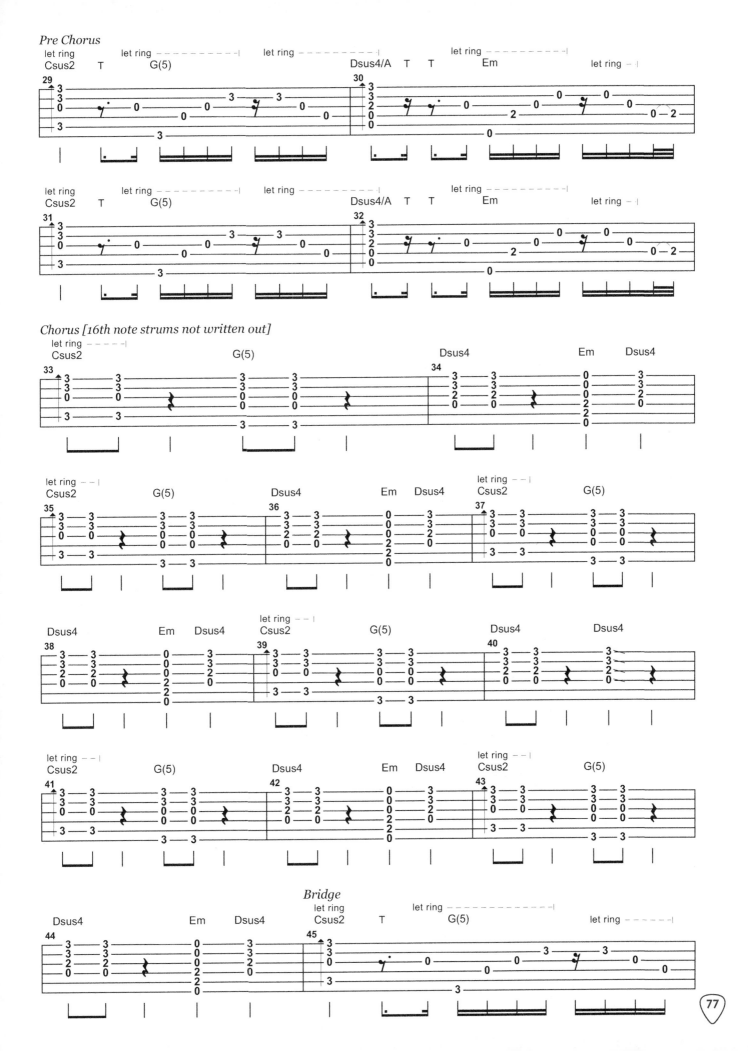

Pre Chorus

Chorus [16th note strums not written out]

Bridge

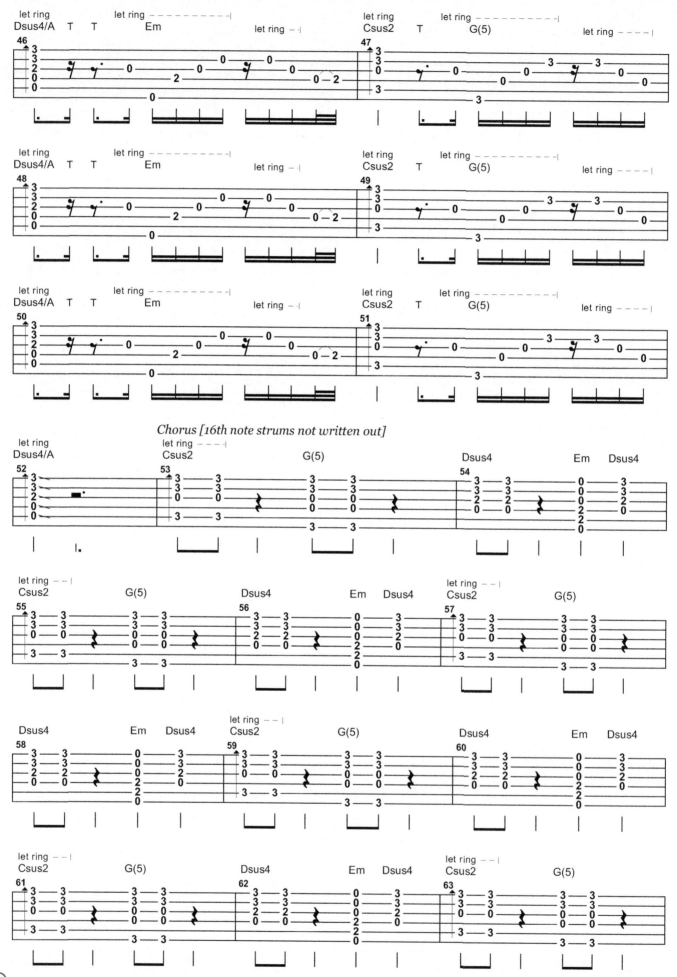

Chorus [16th note strums not written out]

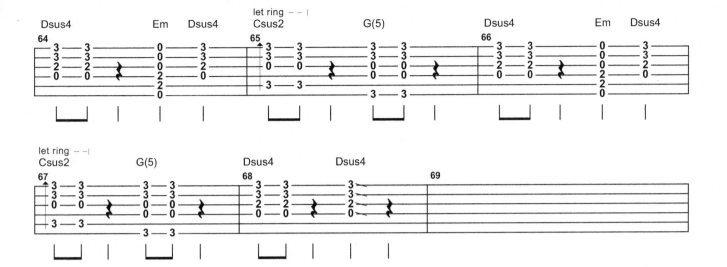

Taylor Swift
All Too Well

Taylor Swift - All Too Well

Track: Acoustic Guitar - Acoustic Guitar (Nylon)

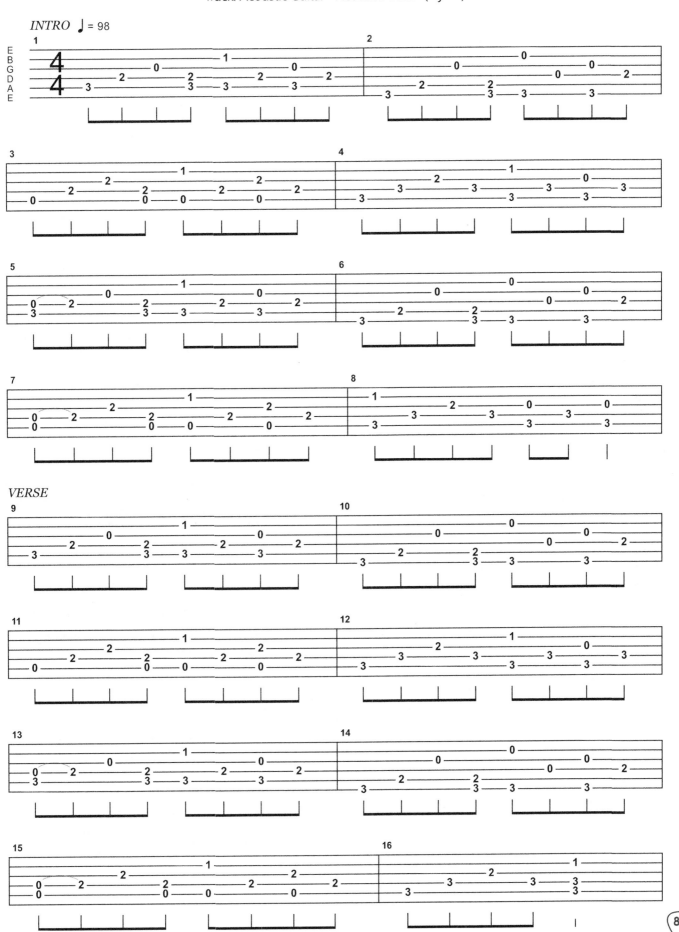

INTERLUDE

VERSE 2

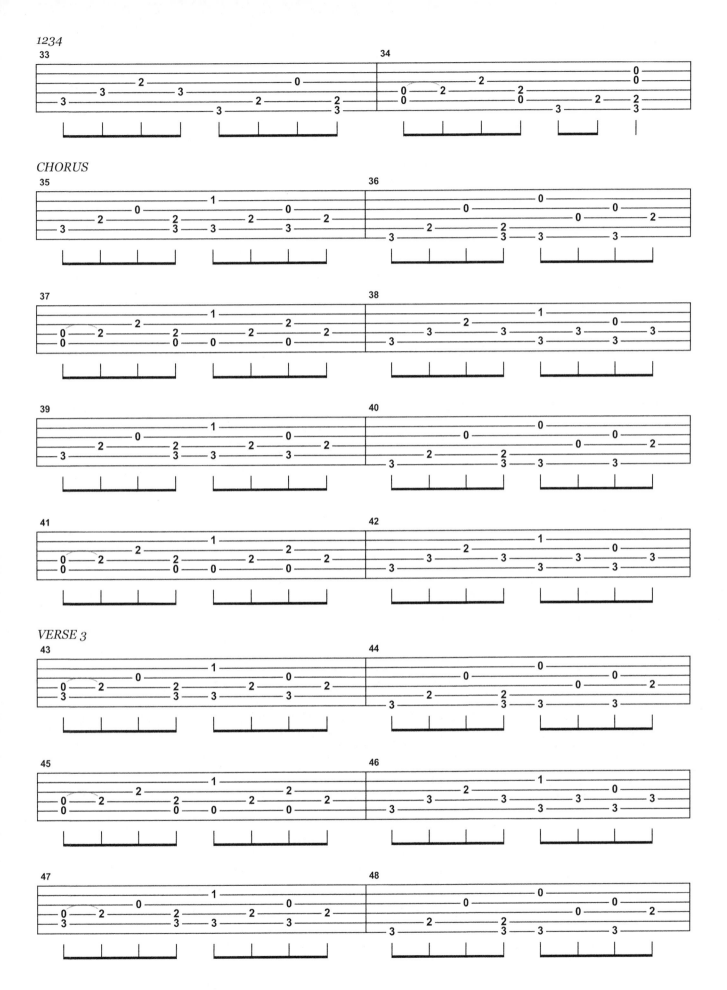

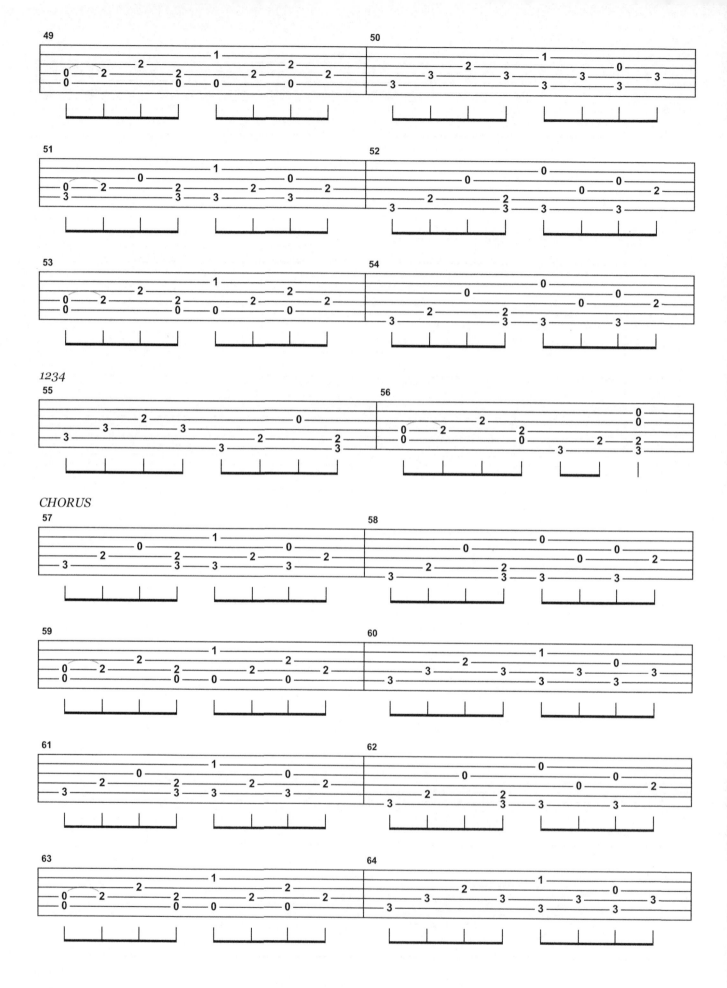

1234

CHORUS

INTERLUDE

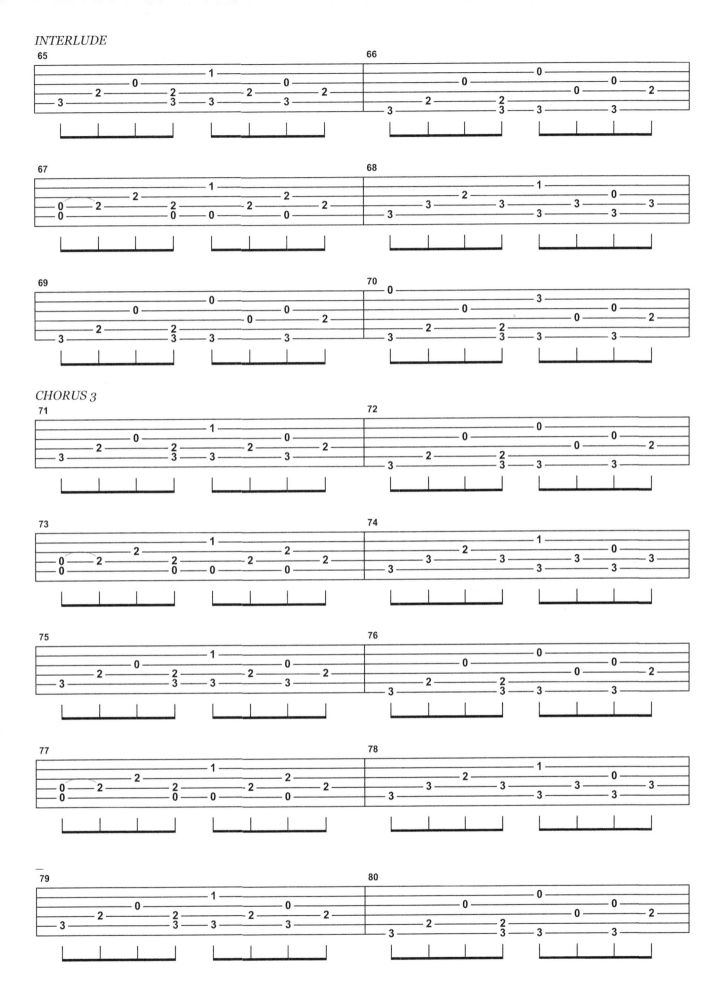

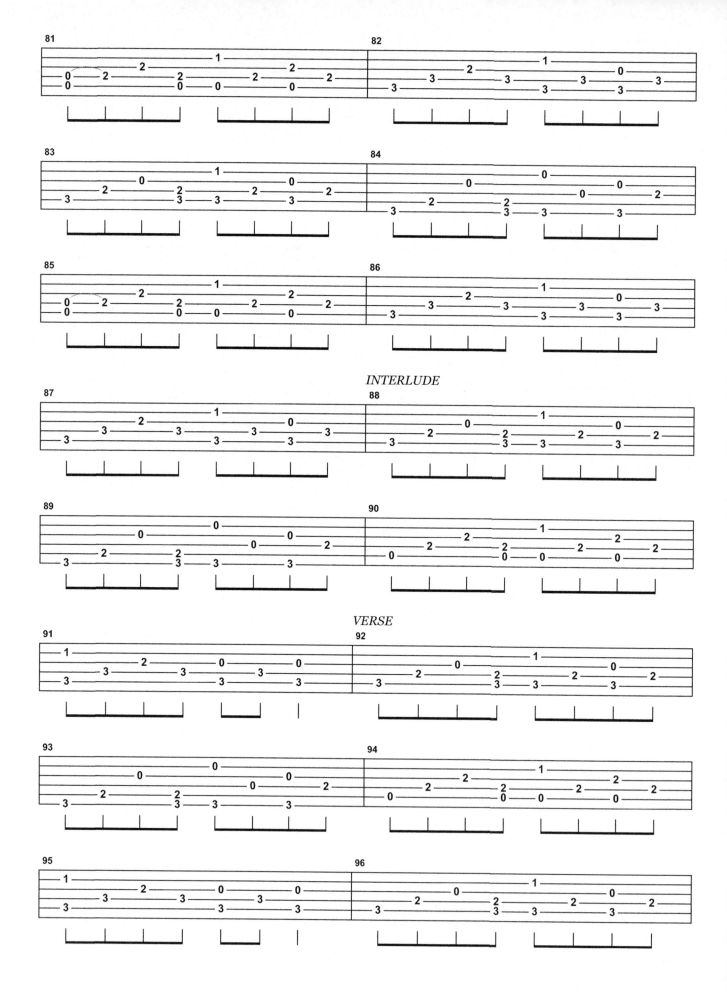

INTERLUDE

VERSE

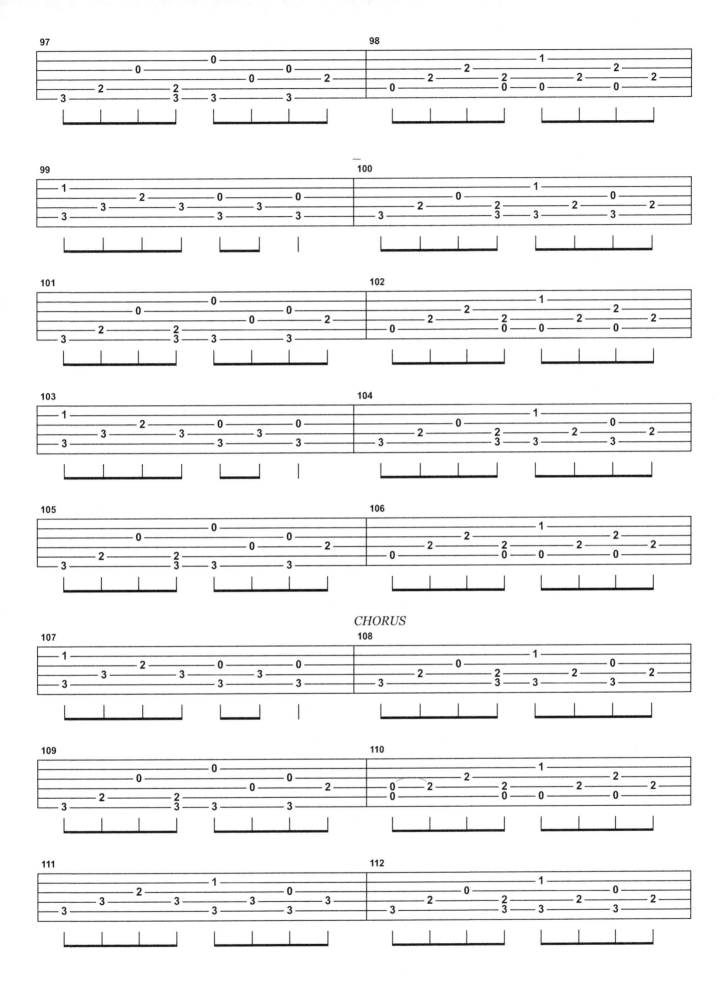

CHORUS

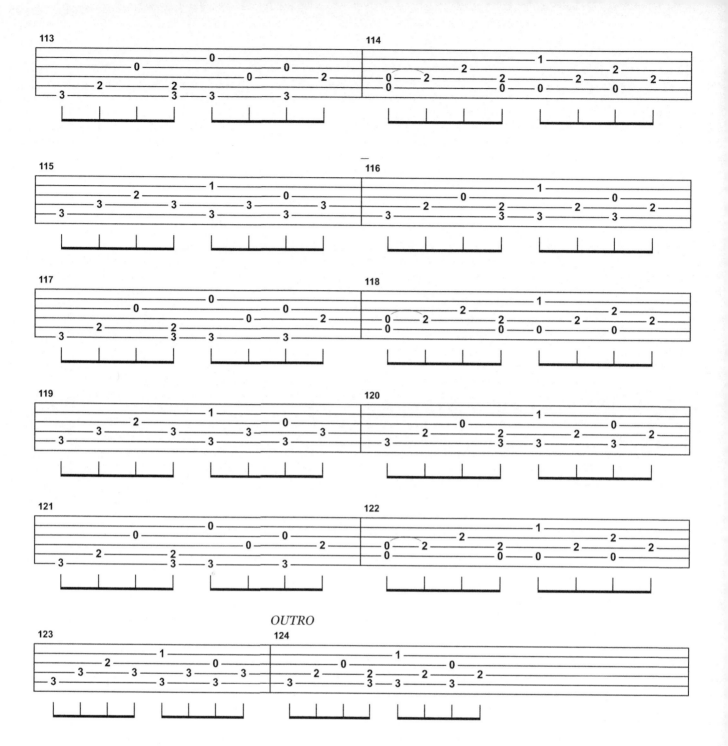

OUTRO

Taylor Swift
Style

Taylor Swift - Style

Track: Clean Guitar 1 - Acoustic Guitar (Steel)

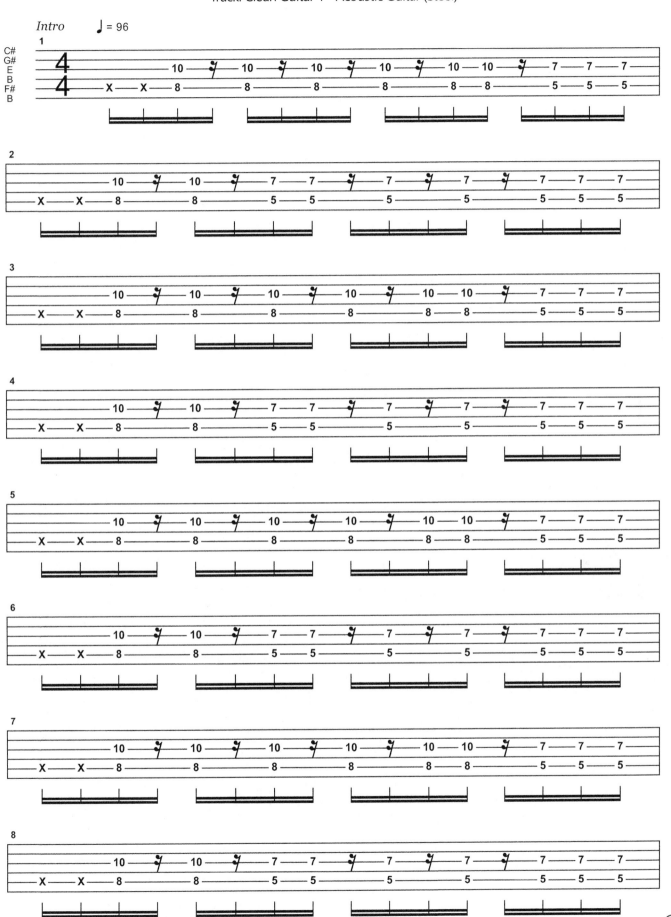

Verse 1

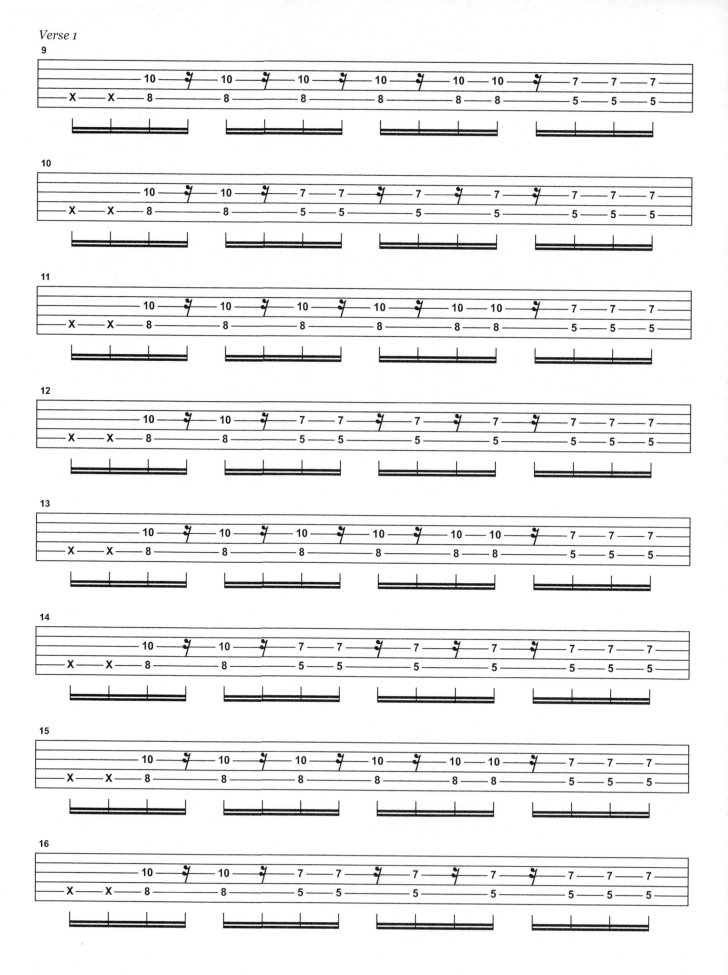

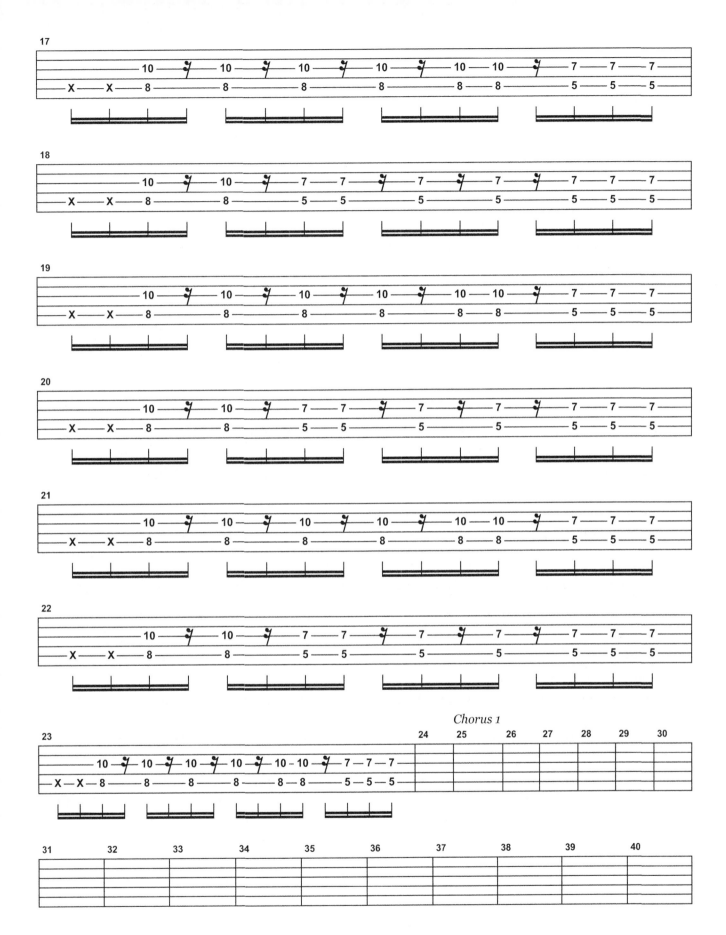

Verse 2

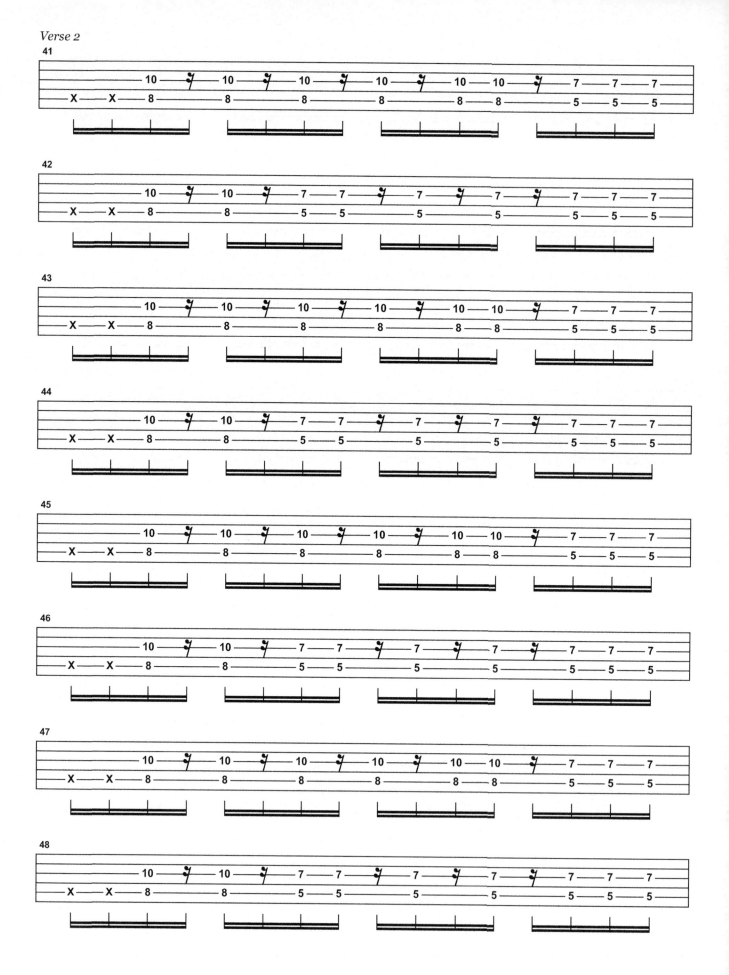

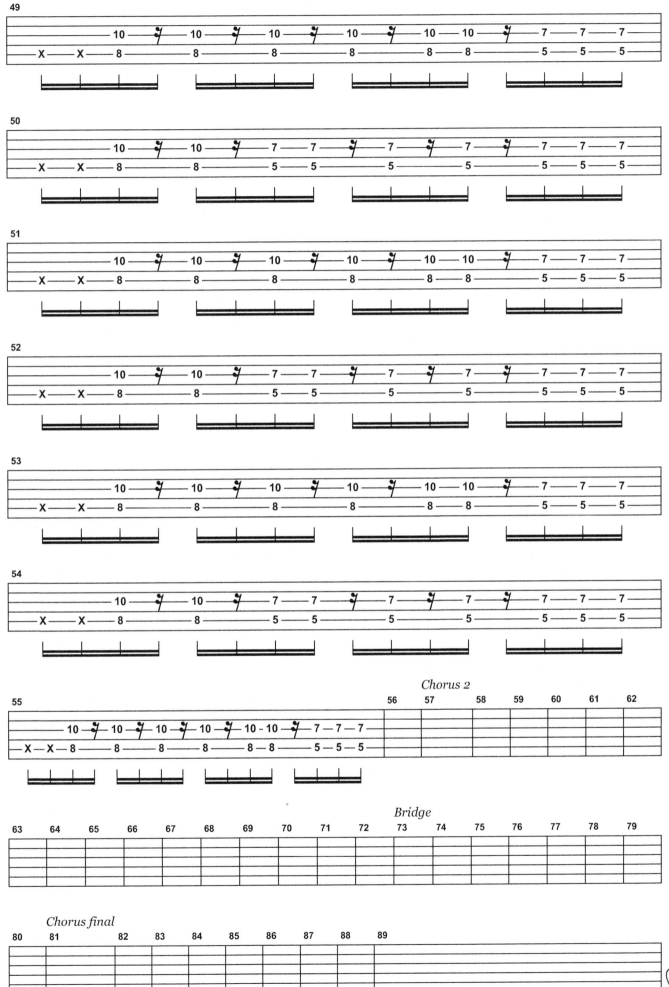

Taylor Swift - Style

Track: Clean Guitar 2 - Acoustic Guitar (Steel)

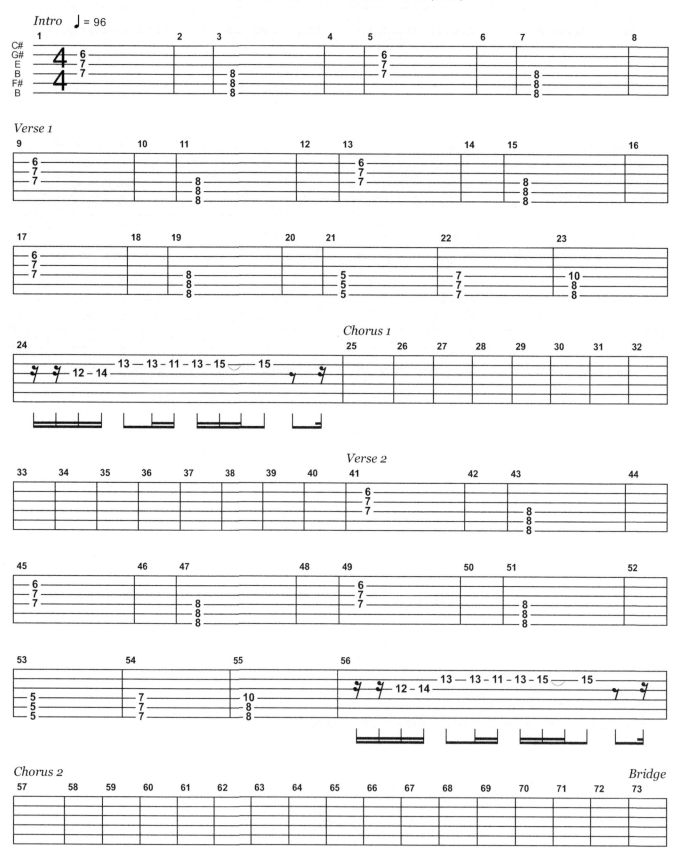

Chorus final

74	75	76	77	78	79	80	81	82	83	84	85	86	87	88	89

Taylor Swift
Blank Space

Taylor Swift - Blank Space

Track: Acoustic - Acoustic Guitar (Steel)

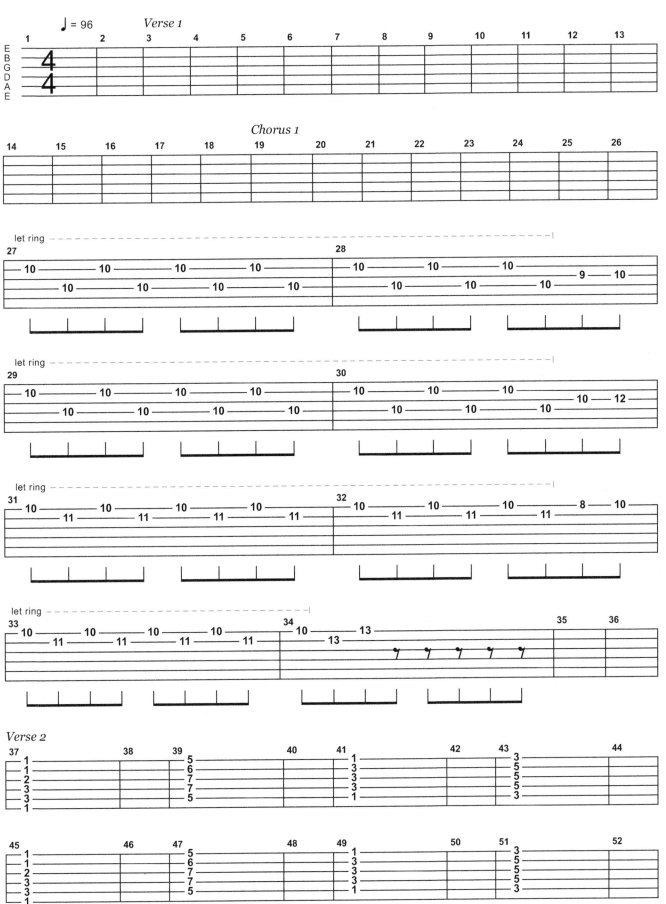

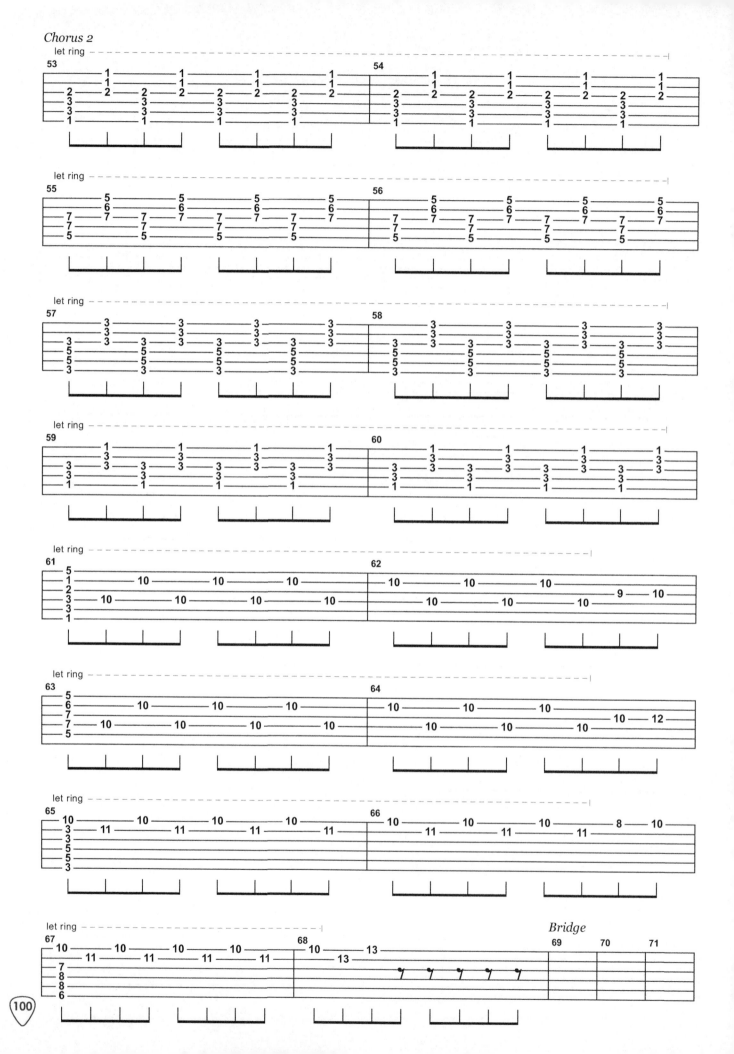

Chorus 3

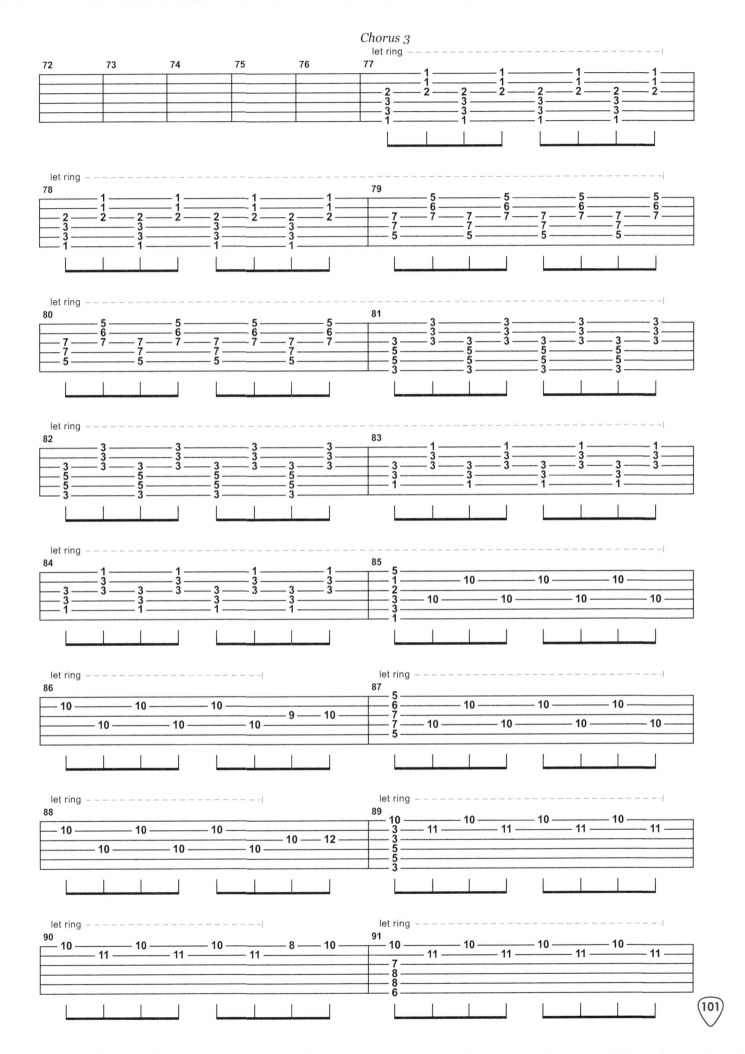

let ring

92
```
|---10-------13-----------------|93-------------------------------------|
|---------13--------------------|-------------------------------------------|
|------------------%--%--%--%--%|-------------------------------------------|
|-------------------------------|-------------------------------------------|
|-------------------------------|-------------------------------------------|
|-------------------------------|-------------------------------------------|
```

Taylor Swift
Fifteen

Taylor Swift - Fifteen

Track: Track 1 - Acoustic Guitar (Nylon)

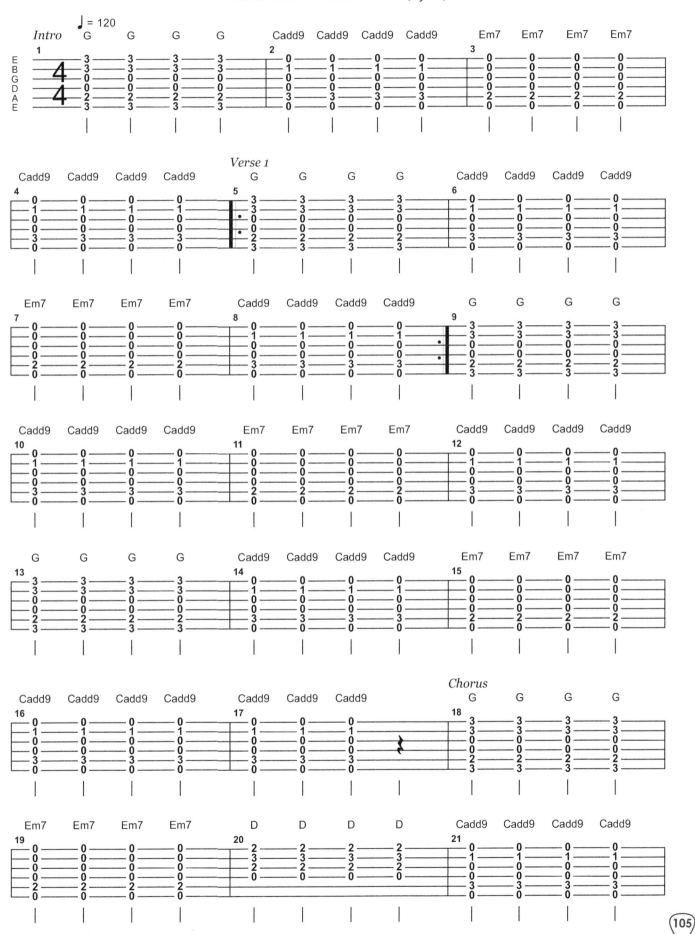

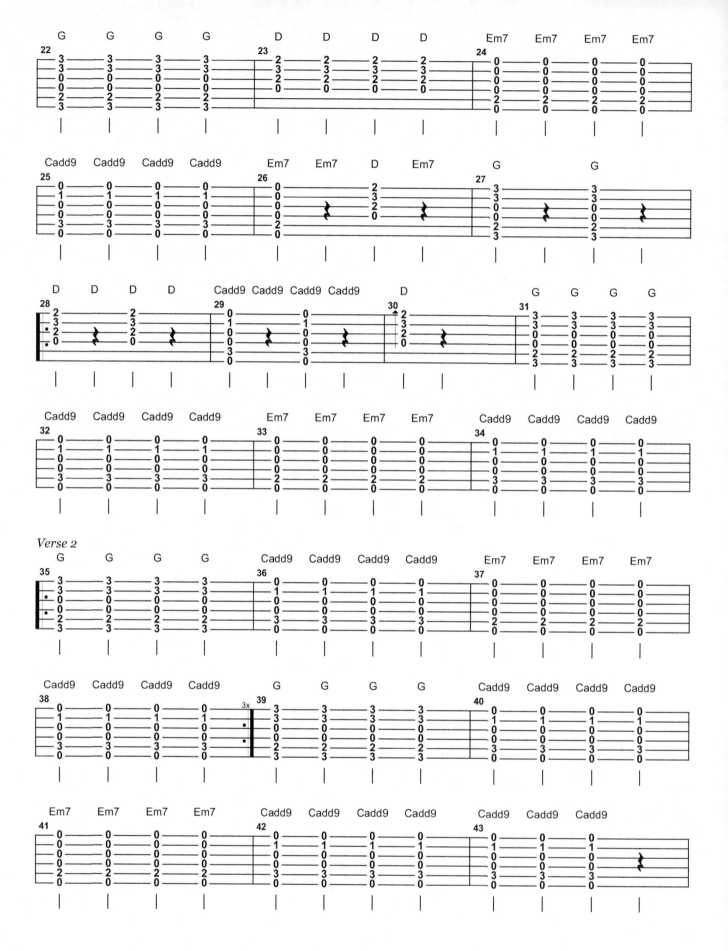

Verse 2

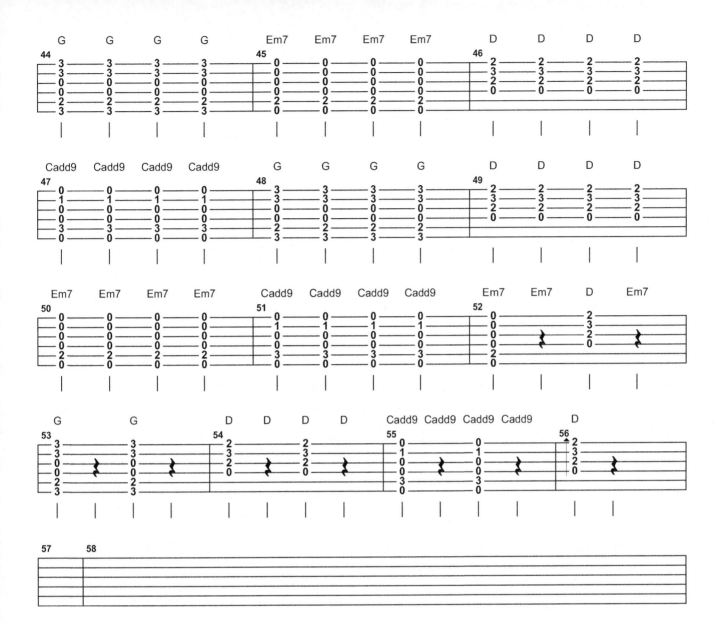

Taylor Swift
Mine

Taylor Swift - Mine

Track: Guitar - Acoustic Guitar (Steel)

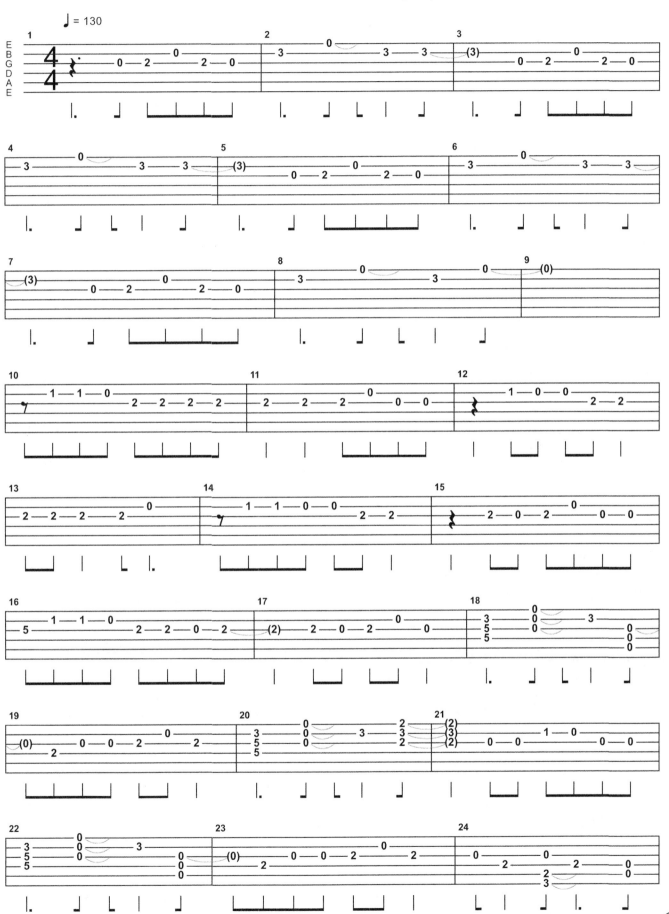

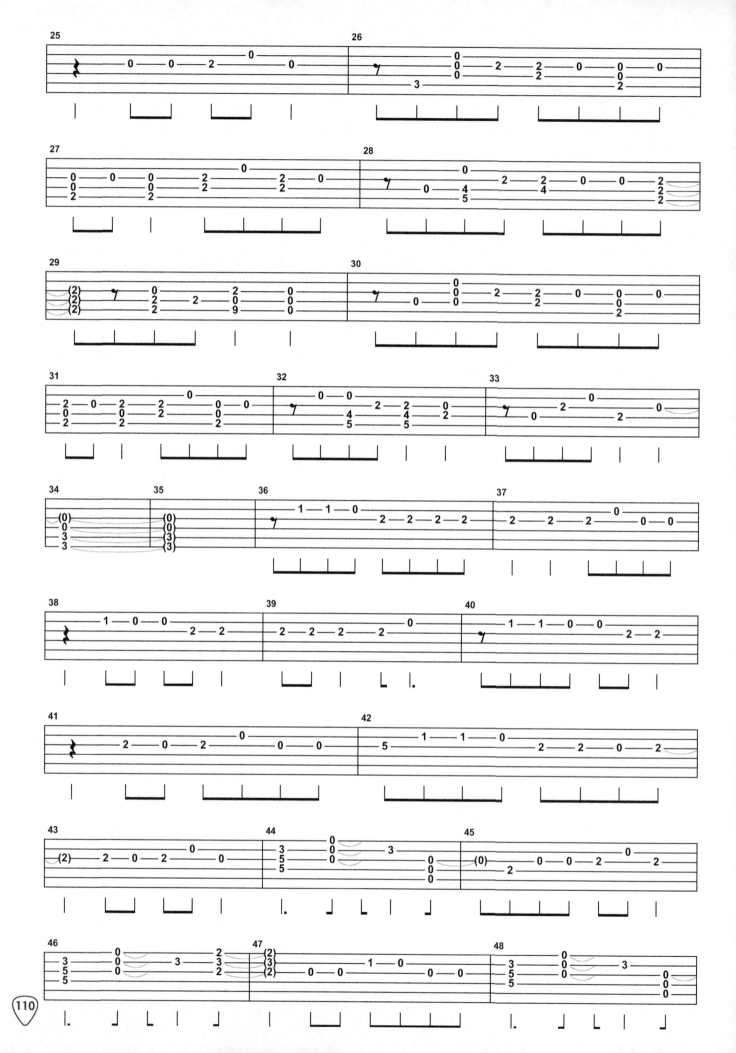

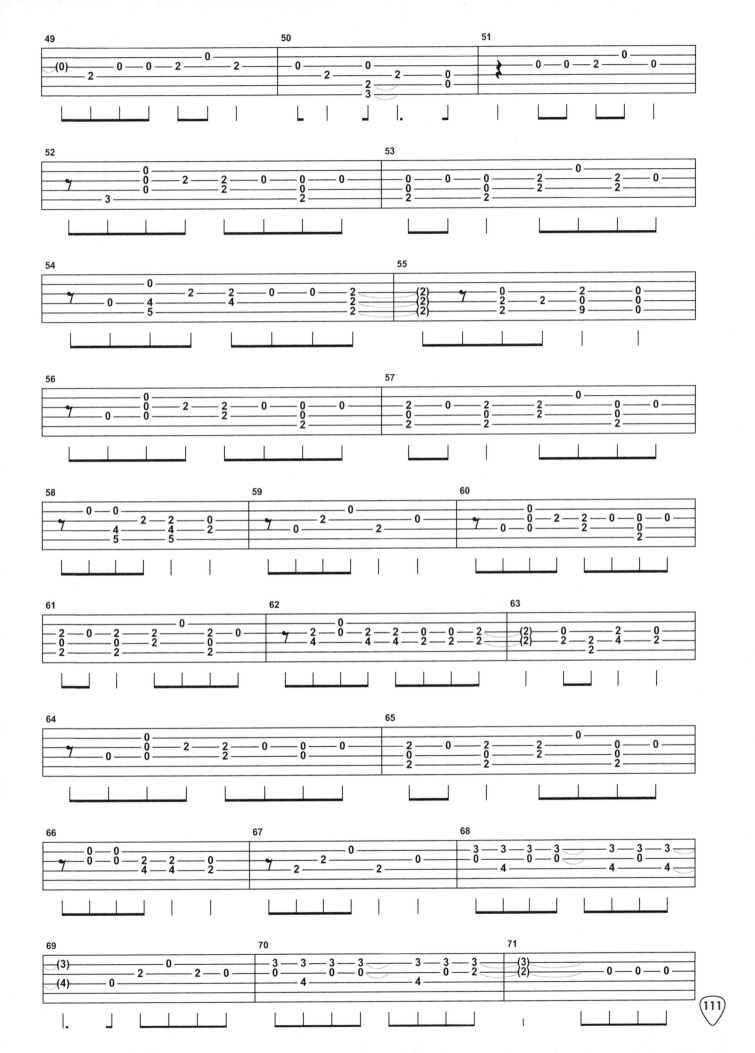

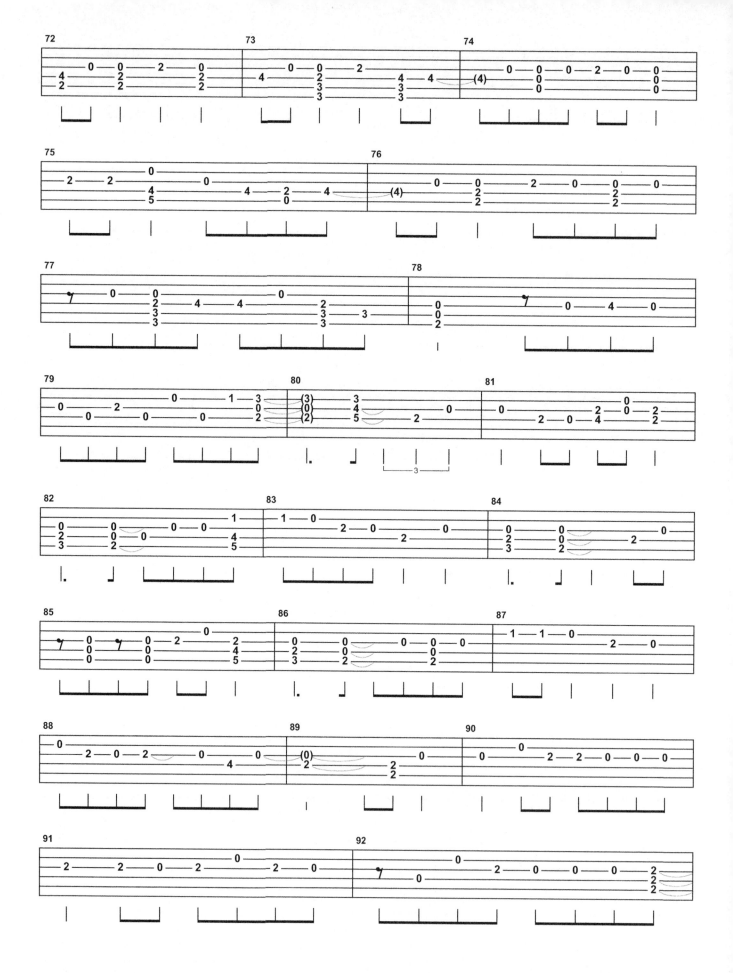

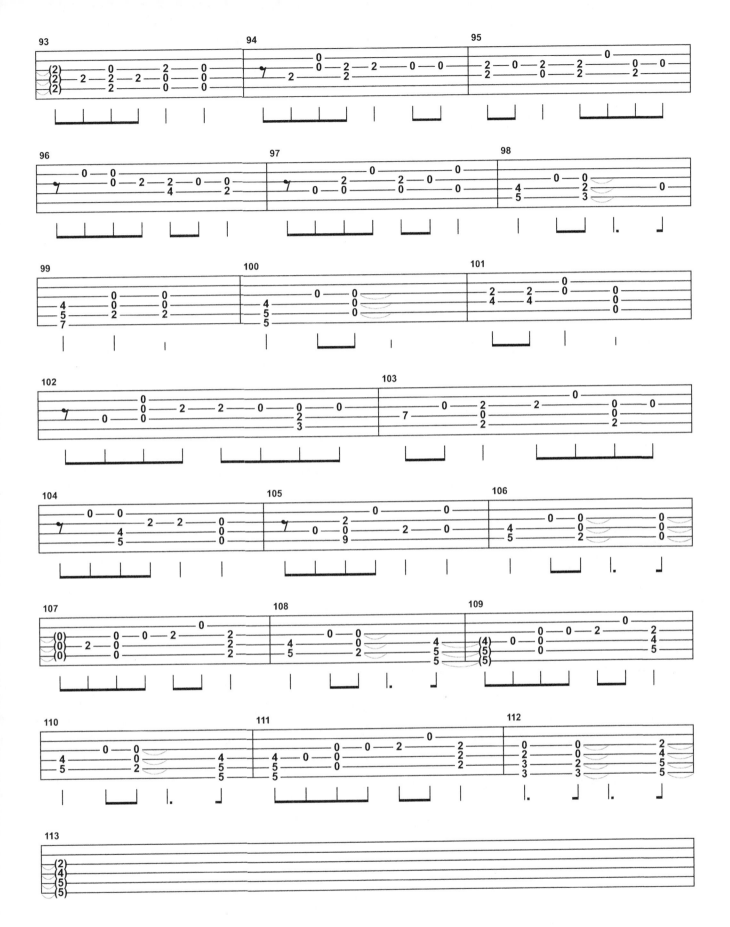

Taylor Swift - Mine

Track: Back-Up Guitar/Vocals - Acoustic Guitar (Steel)

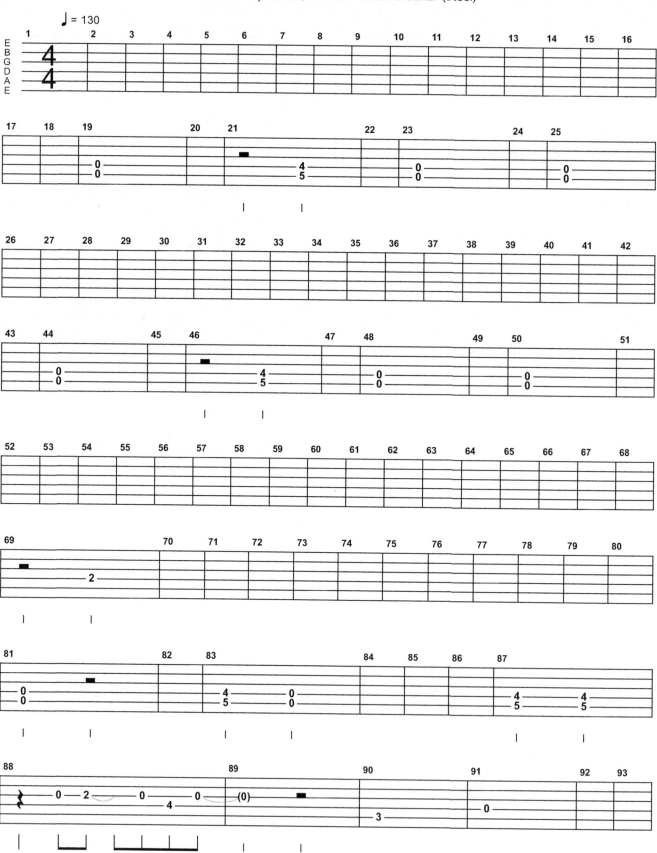

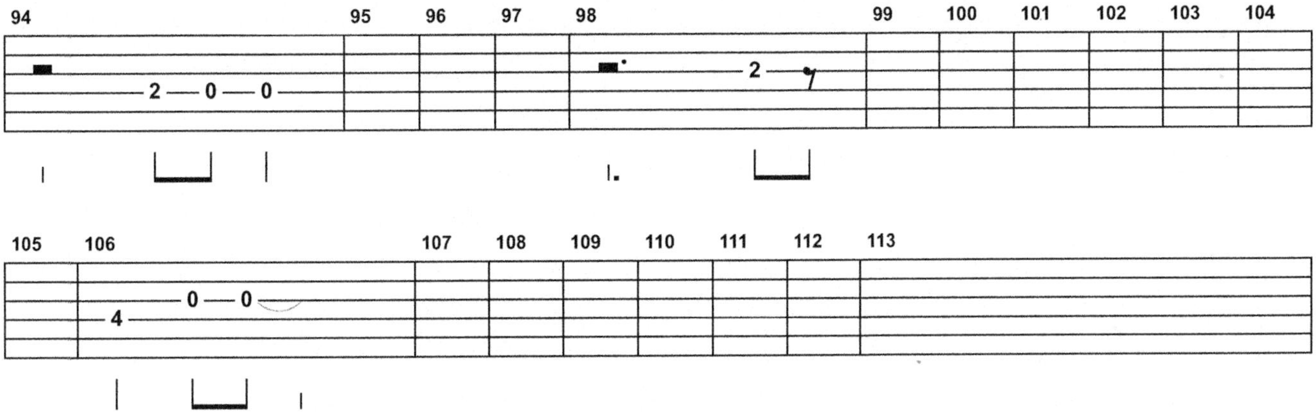

Taylor Swift

Picture To Burn

Taylor Swift - Picture To Burn

Track: Steel Guitar - Acoustic Guitar (Steel)

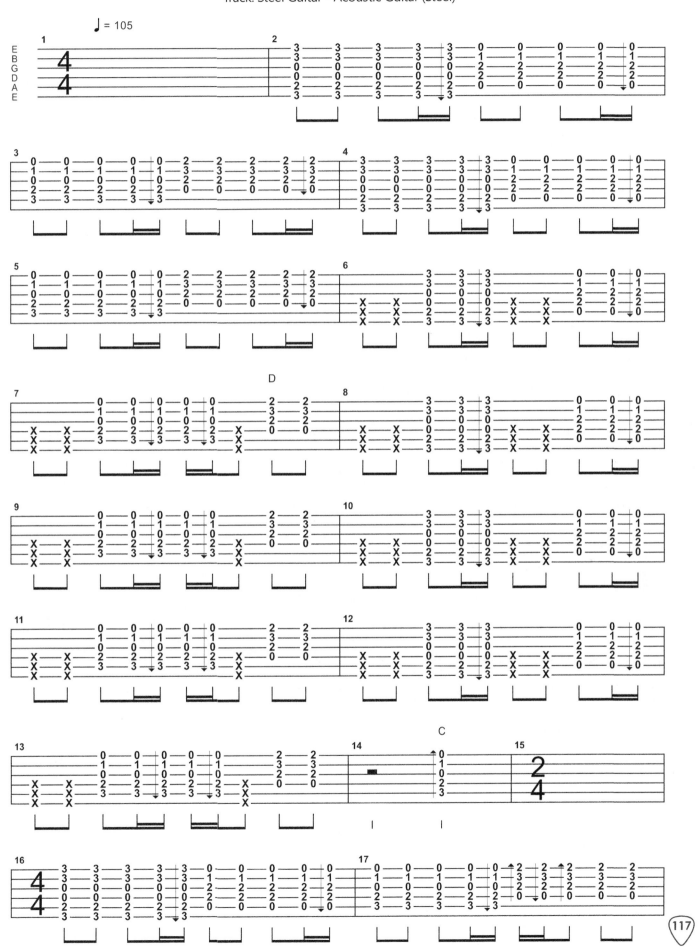

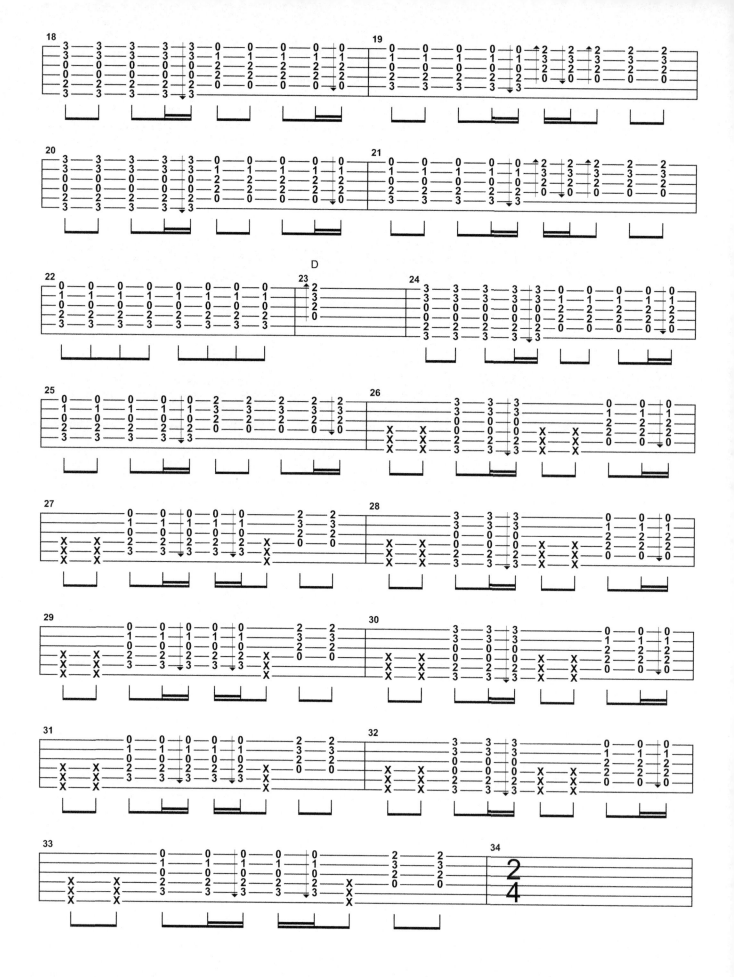

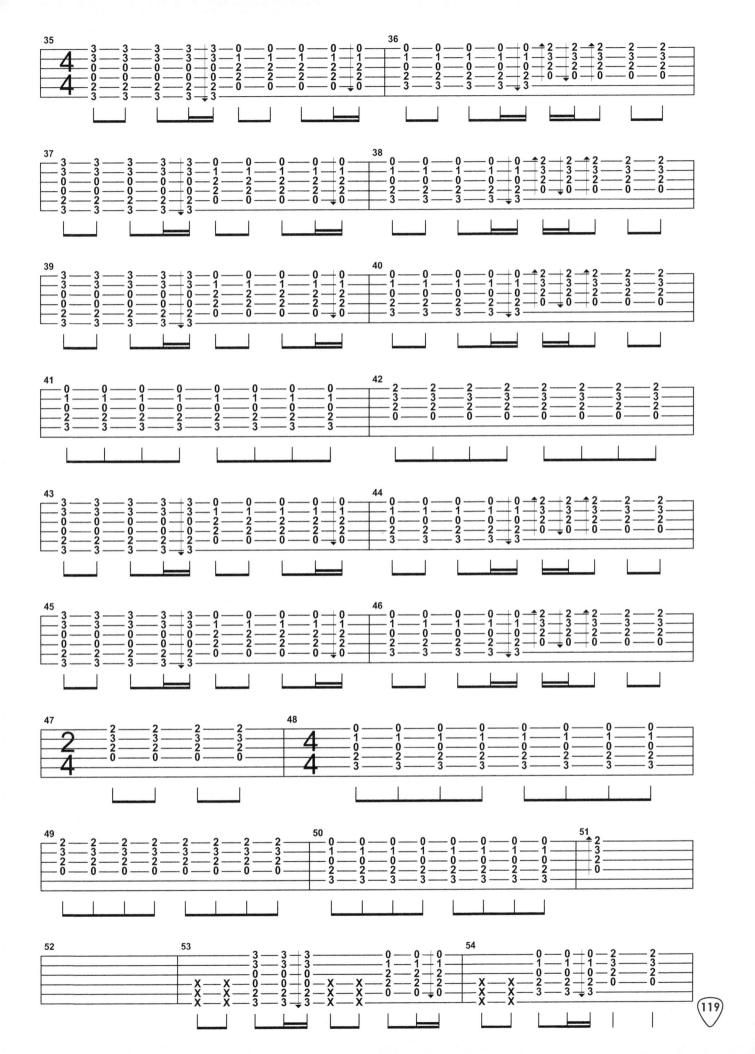

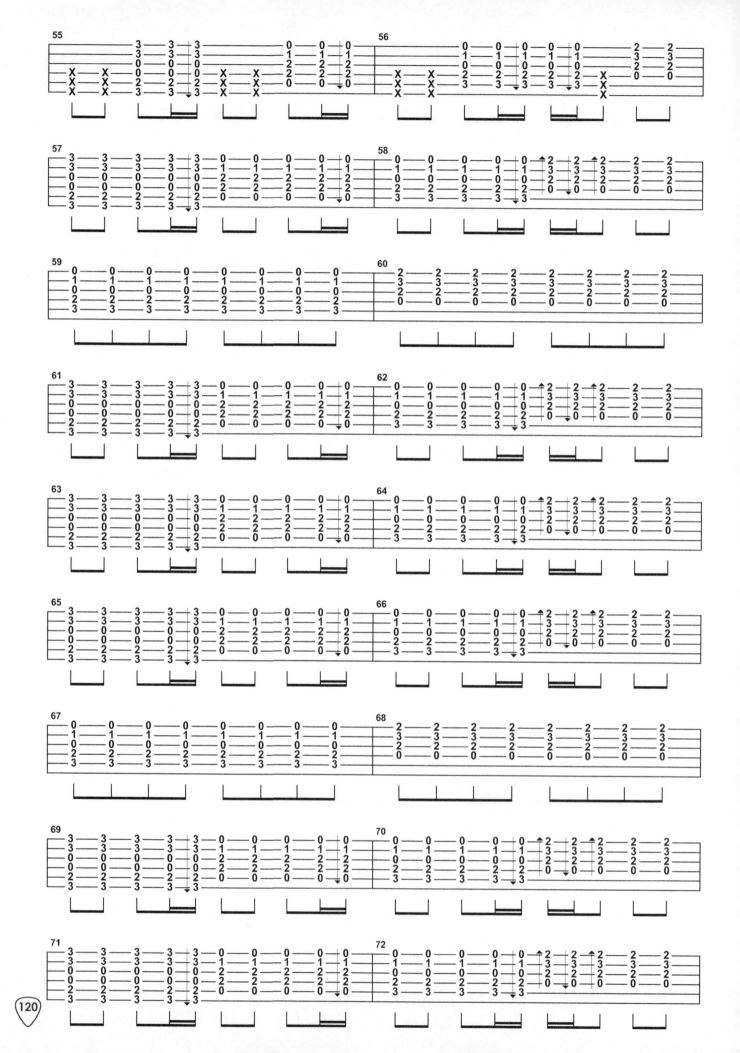

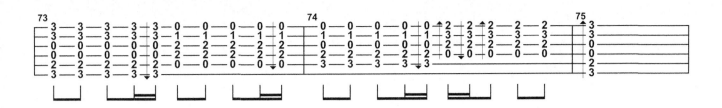

Taylor Swift
Safe And Sound

Taylor Swift - Safe And Sound 1

Track: Ňôšě 1 - Acoustic Guitar (Steel)

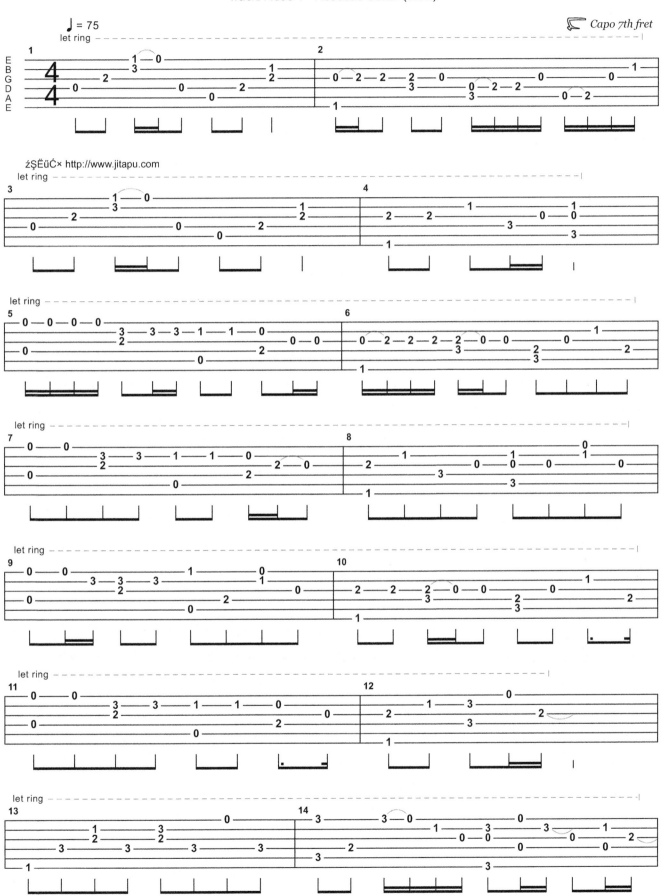

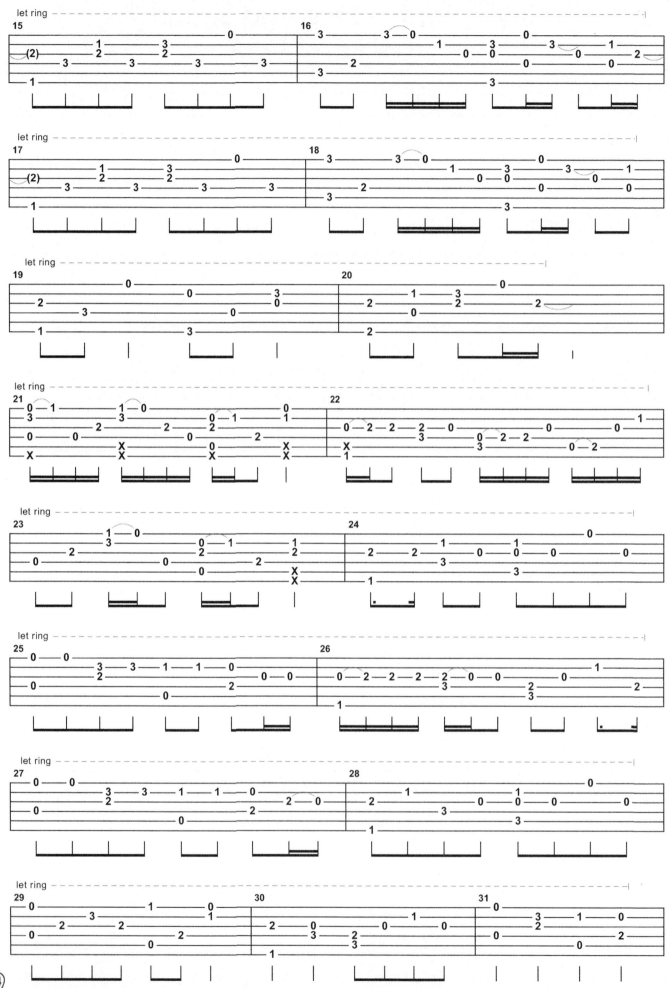

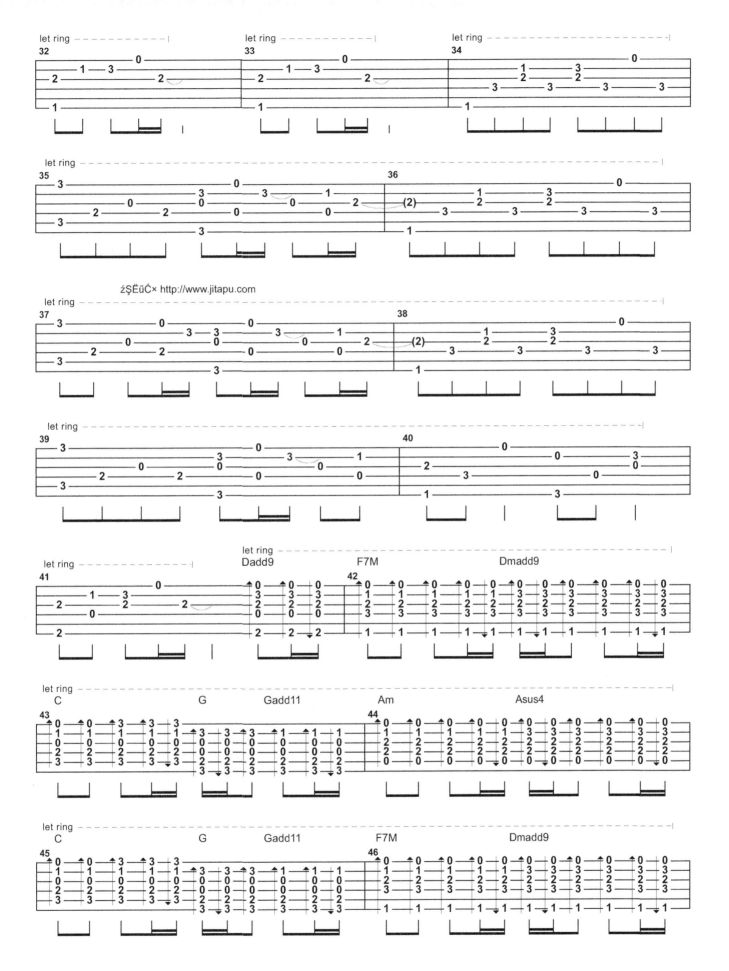

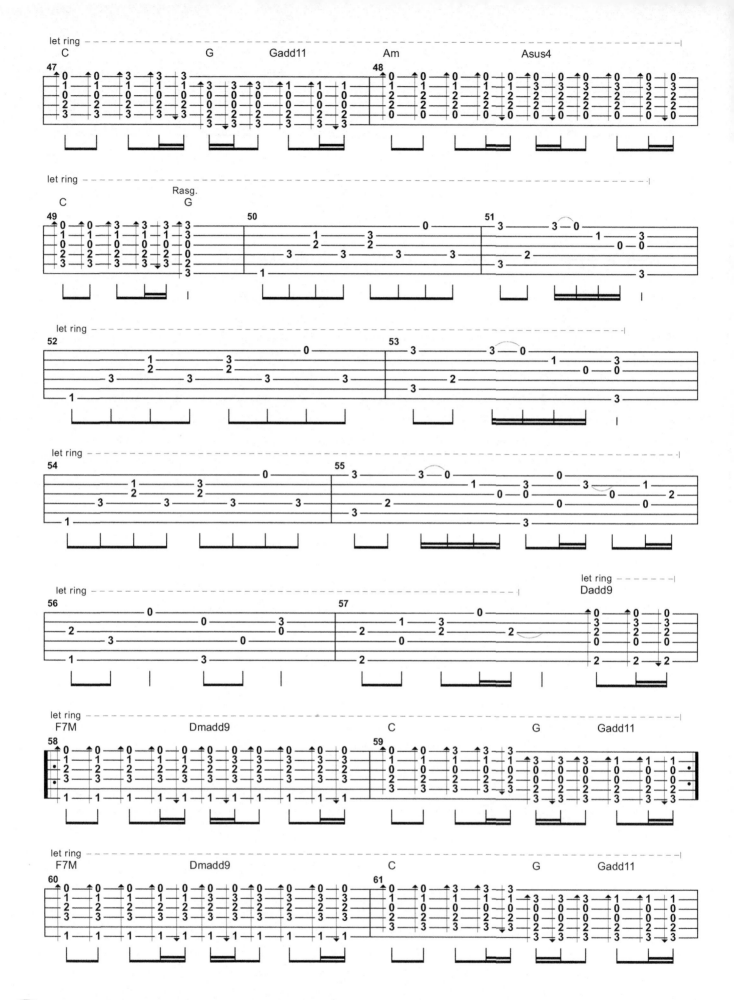

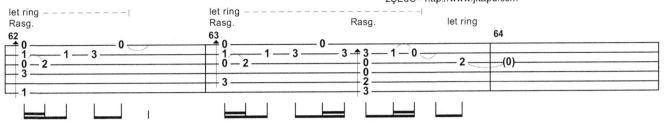

Taylor Swift - Safe And Sound Tab

Track: Chord - Acoustic Guitar (Steel)

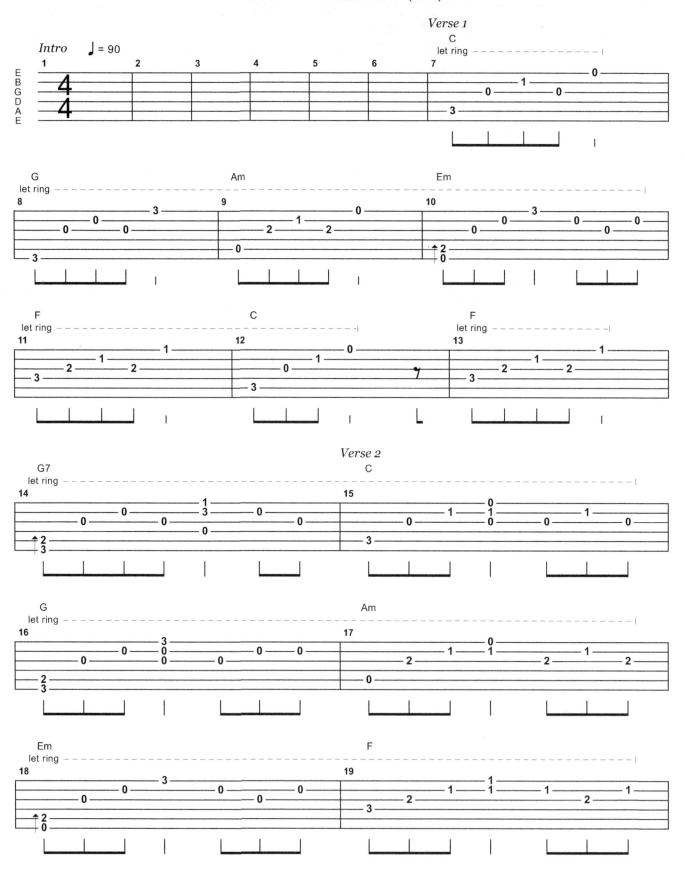

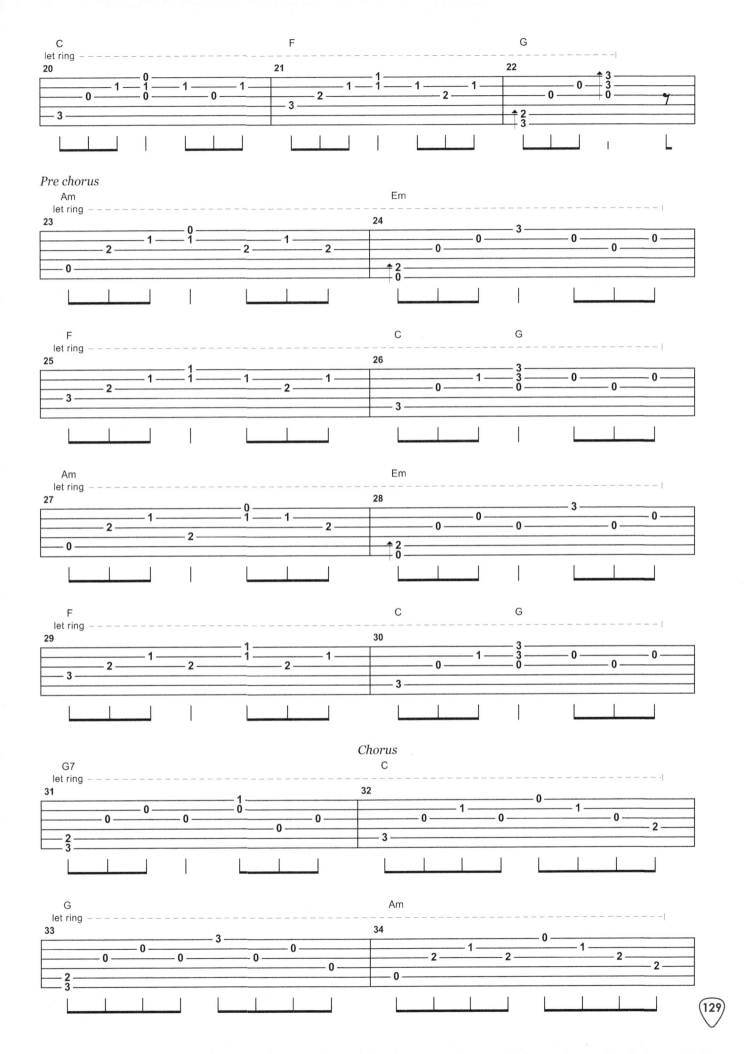

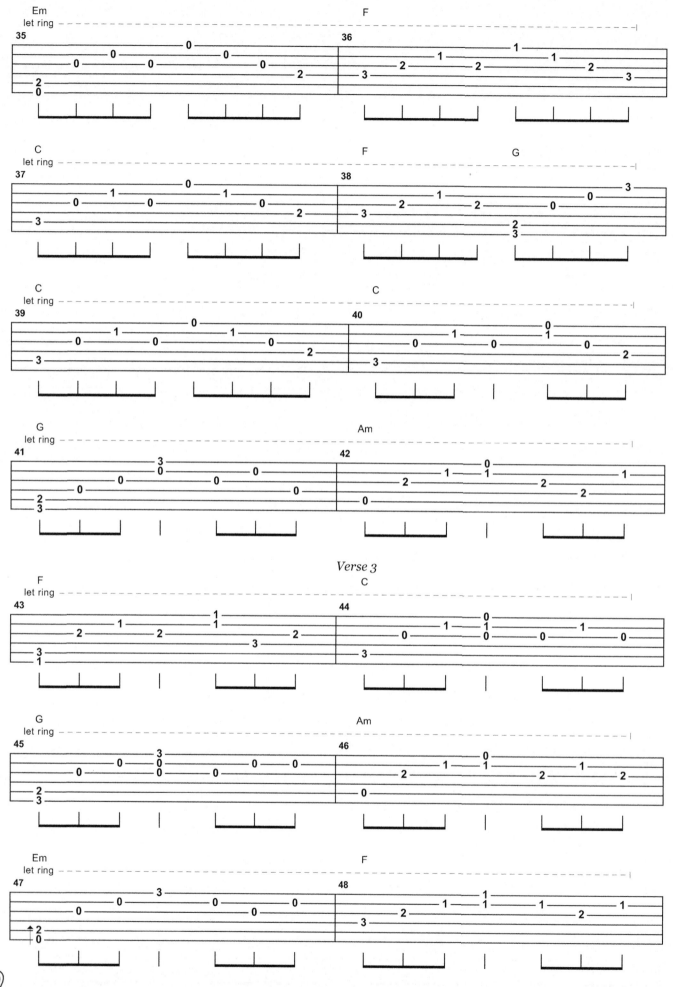

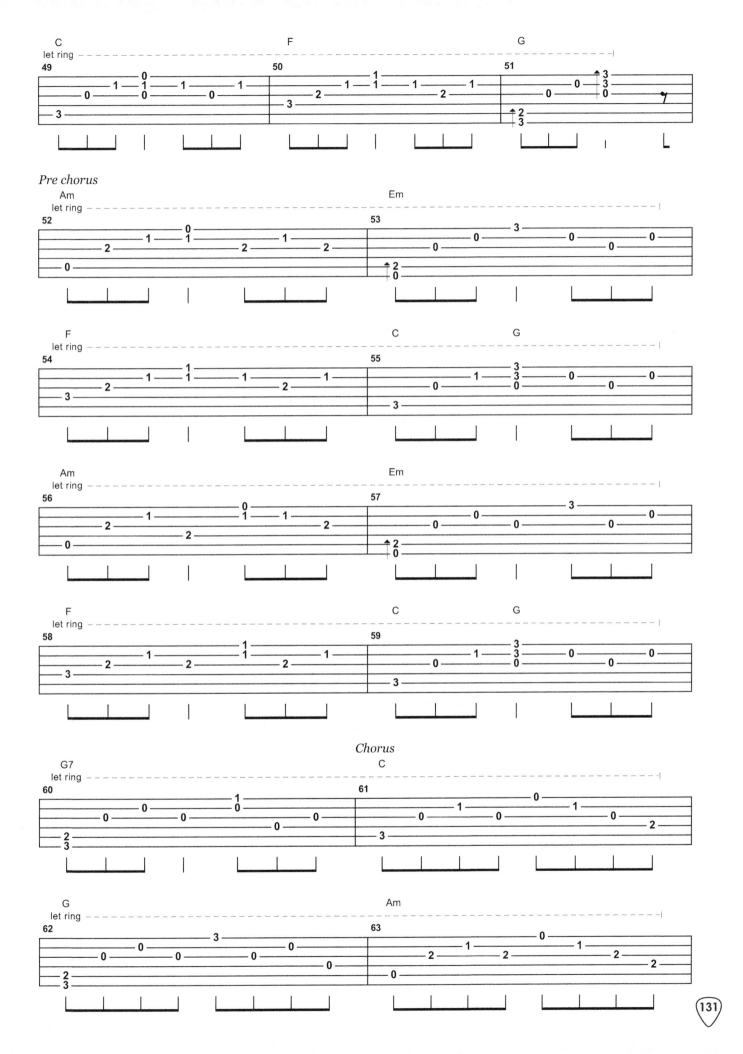

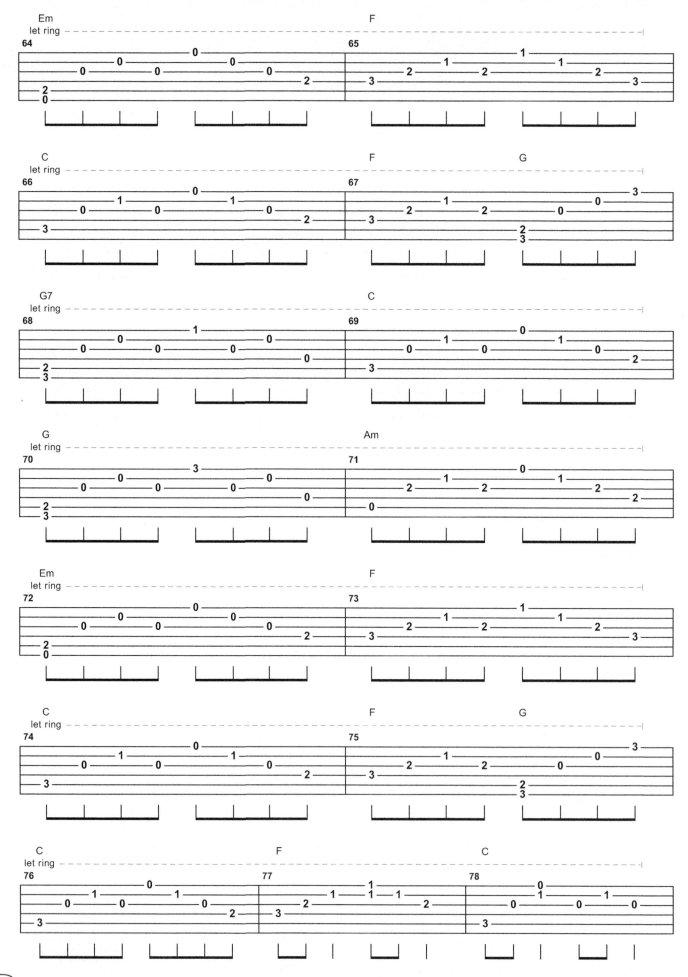

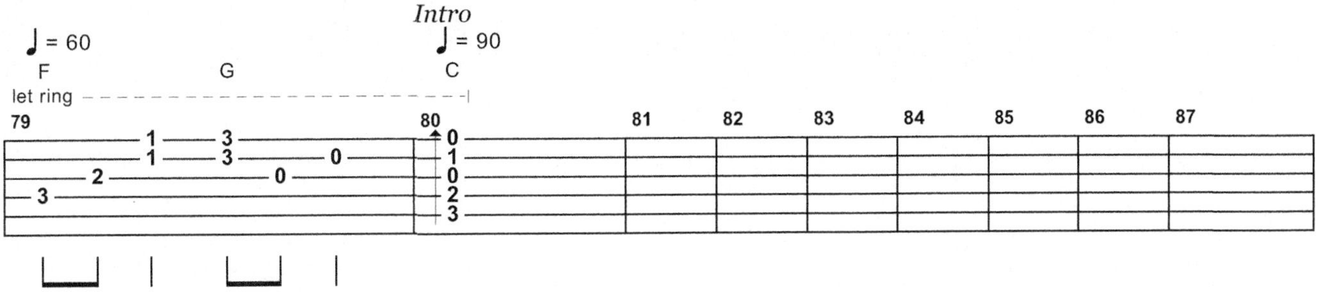
Intro
= 60
= 90
F
G
C
let ring
79
80
81
82
83
84
85
86
87

Taylor Swift

Teardrops On My Guitar

Taylor Swift - Teardrops On My Guitar

Track: Track 1 - Acoustic Guitar (Nylon)

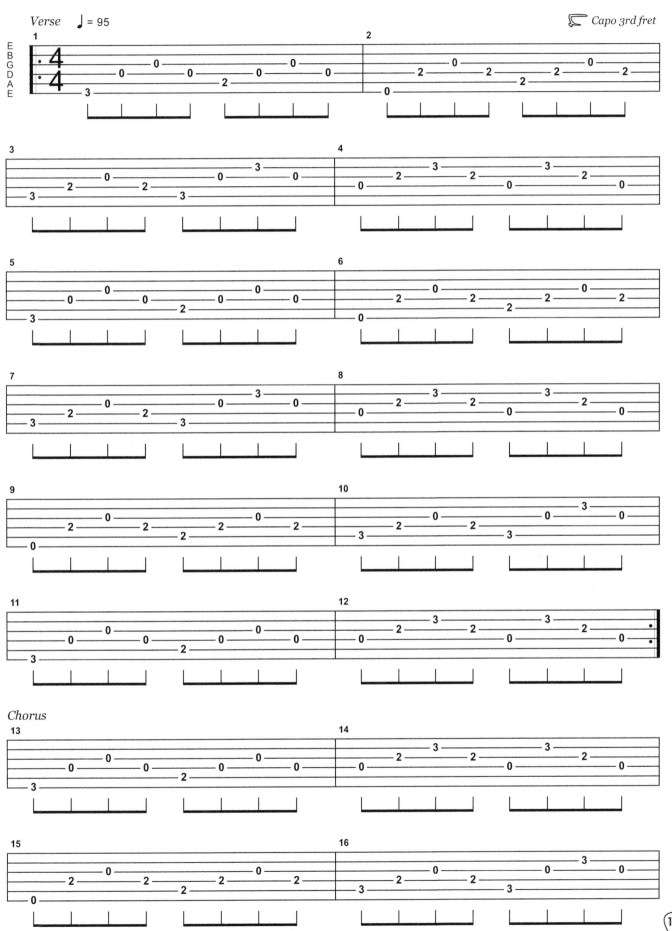

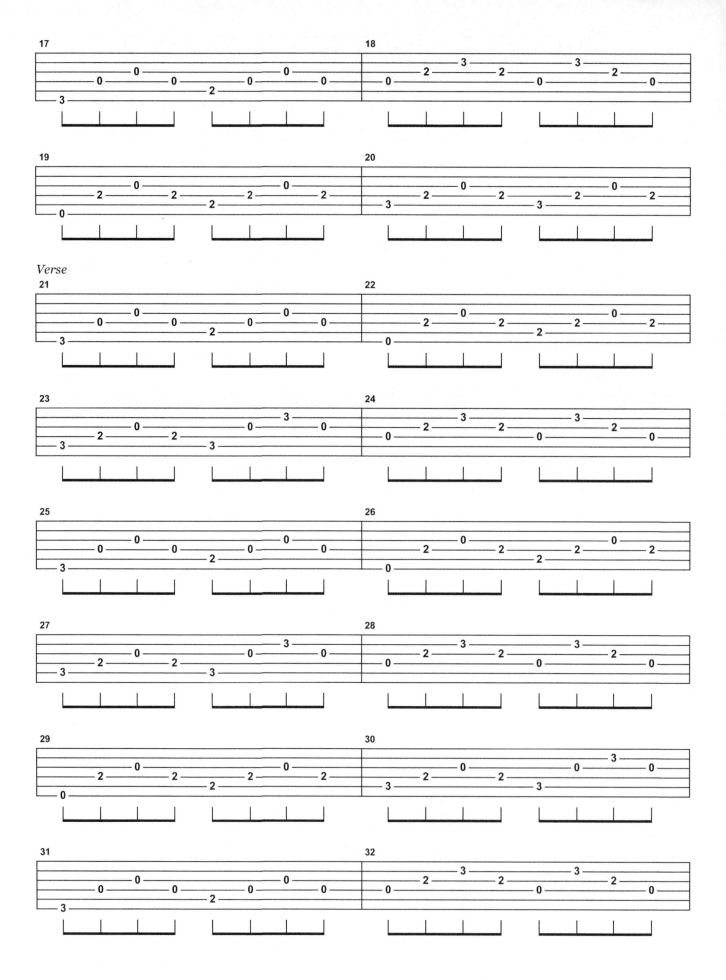

Chorus

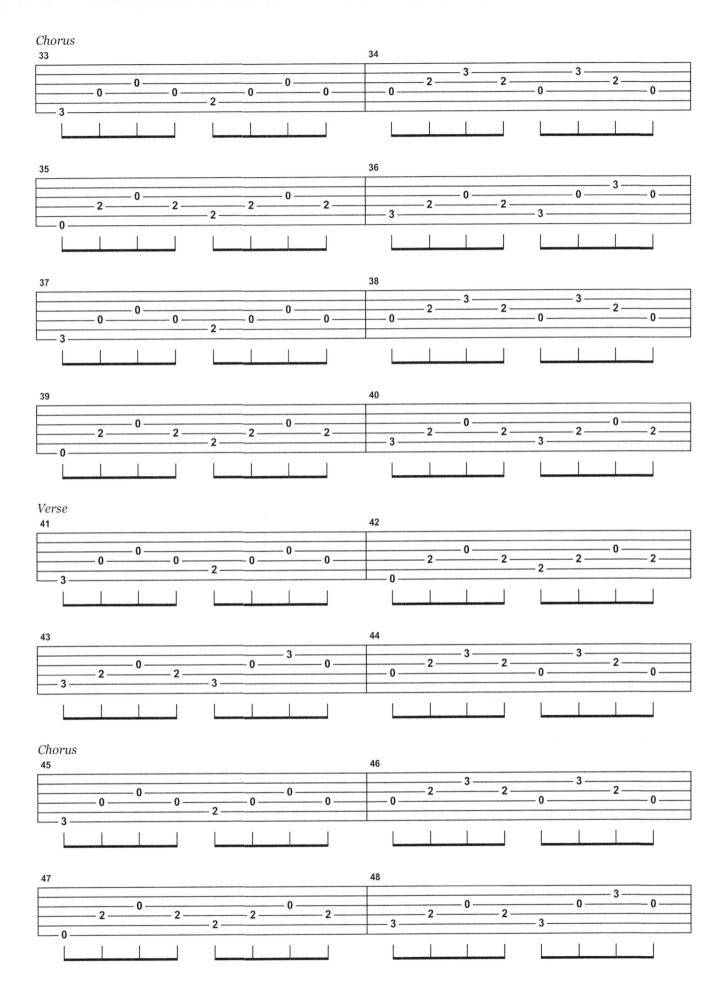

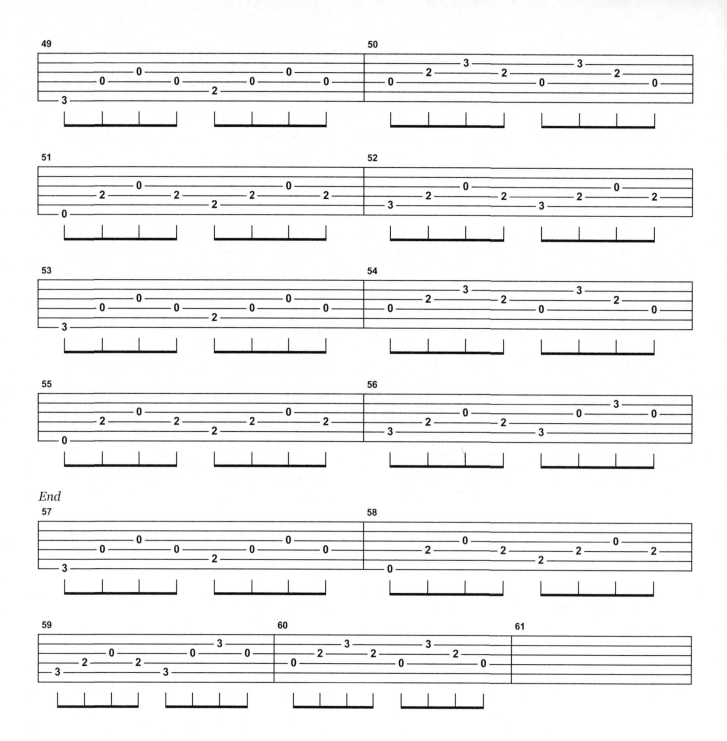

End

Taylor Swift - Teardrops On My Guitar

Track: Track 2 - Acoustic Guitar (Steel)

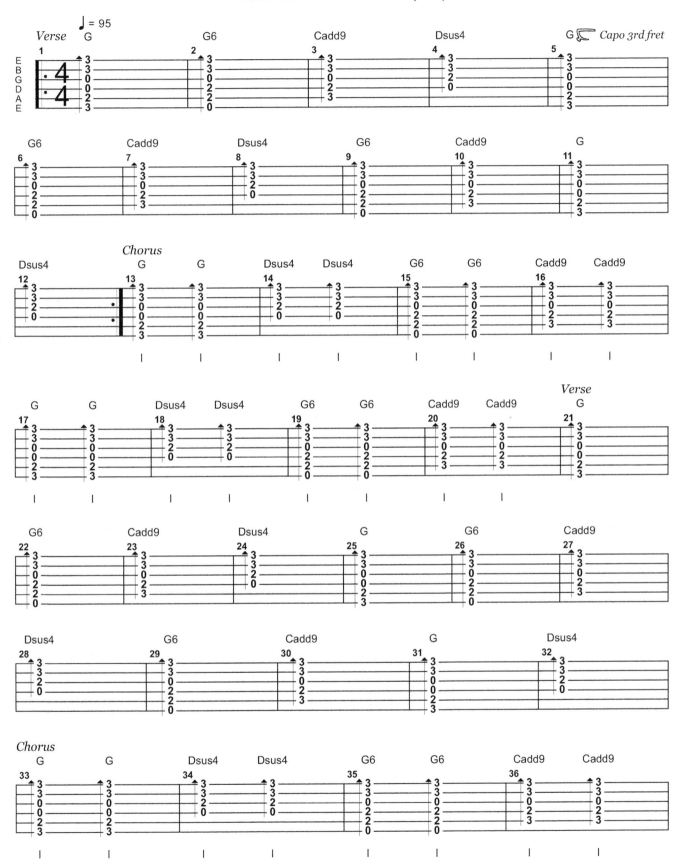

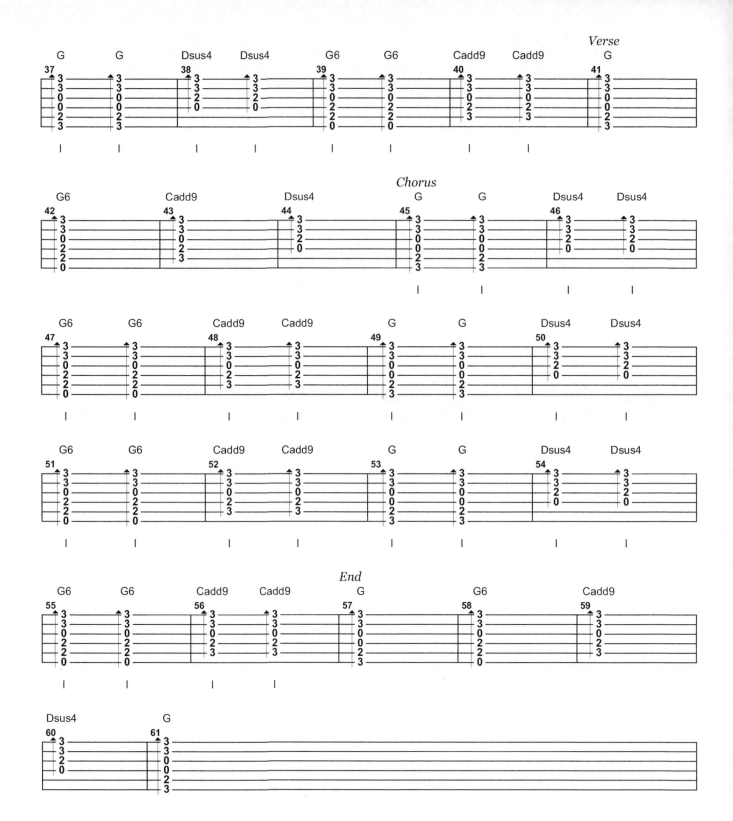

Taylor Swift
White Horse

Taylor Swift - White Horse

Track: Track 1 - Acoustic Guitar (Steel)

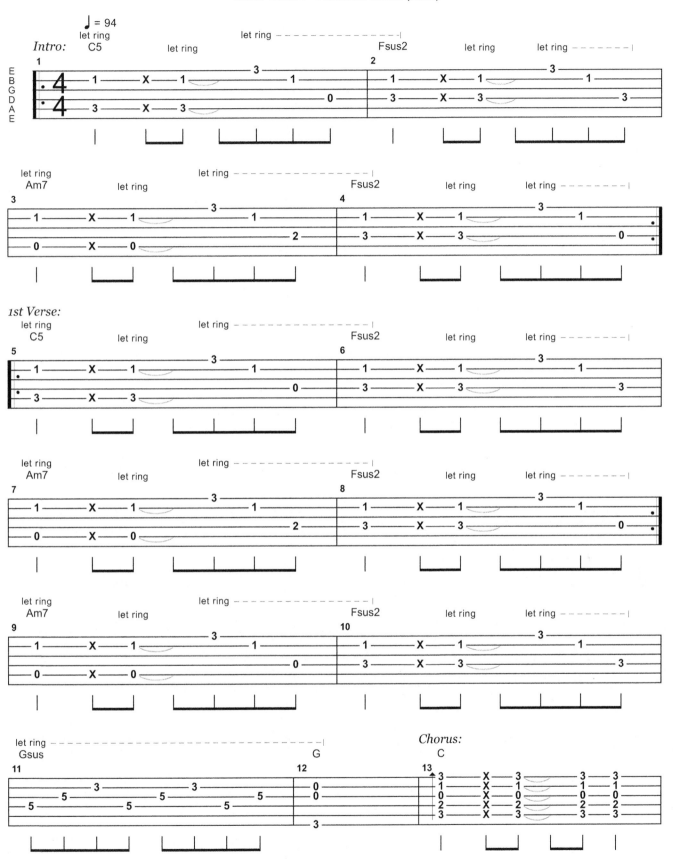

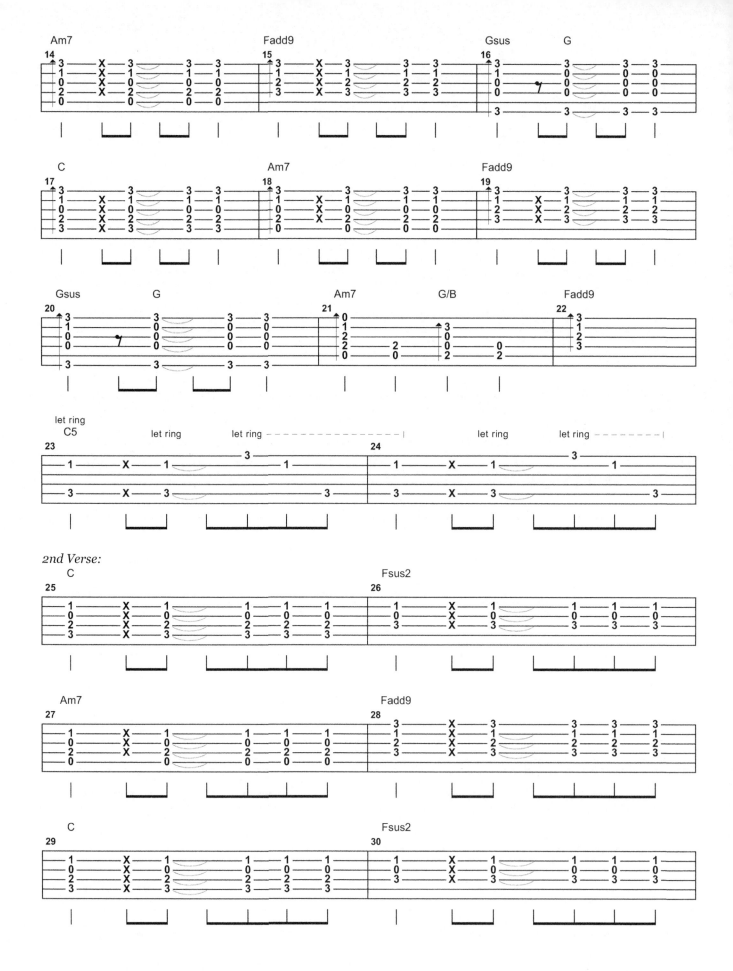

2nd Verse:

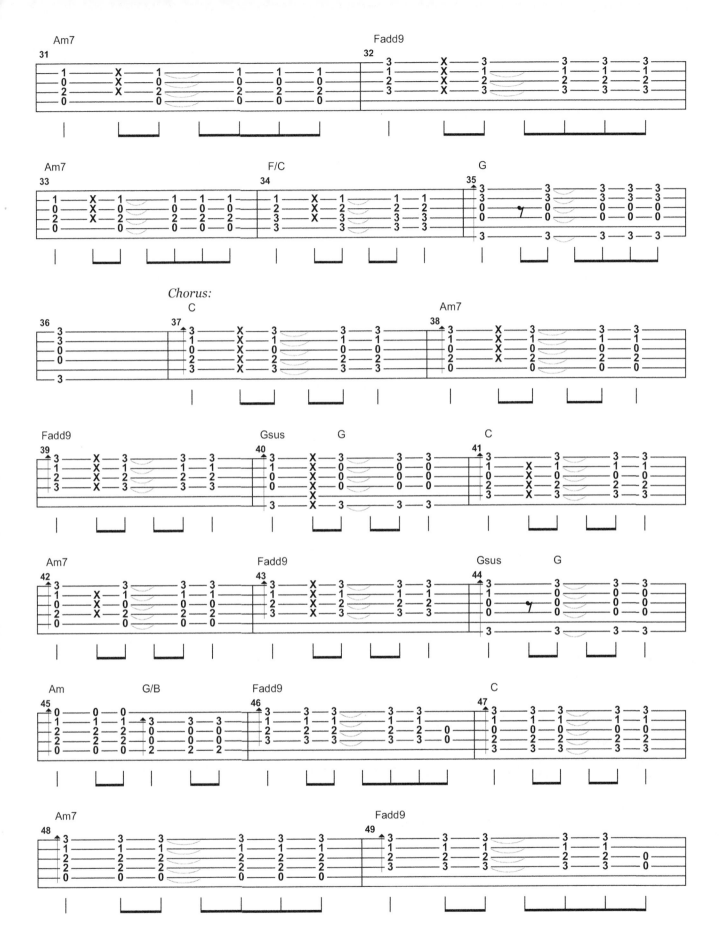

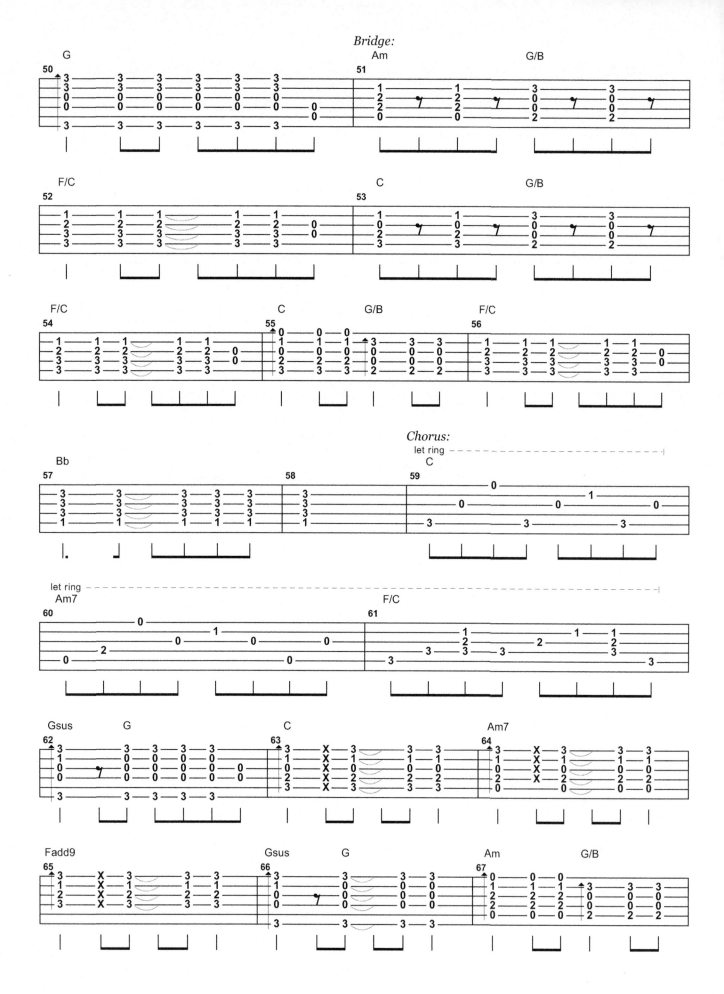

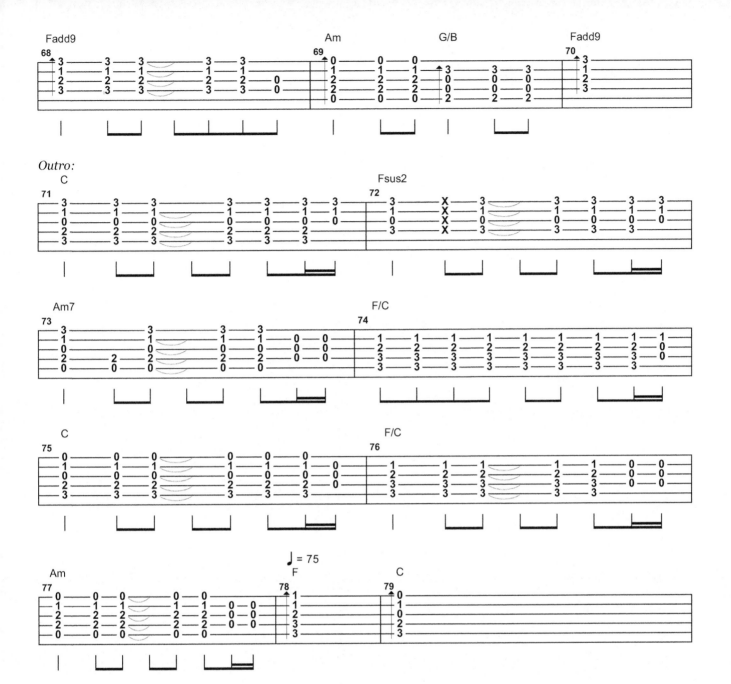

Taylor Swift
Wildest Dreams Fingerstyle

Taylor Swift - Wildest Dreams Fingerstyle

Track: Steel Guitar - Acoustic Guitar (Steel)

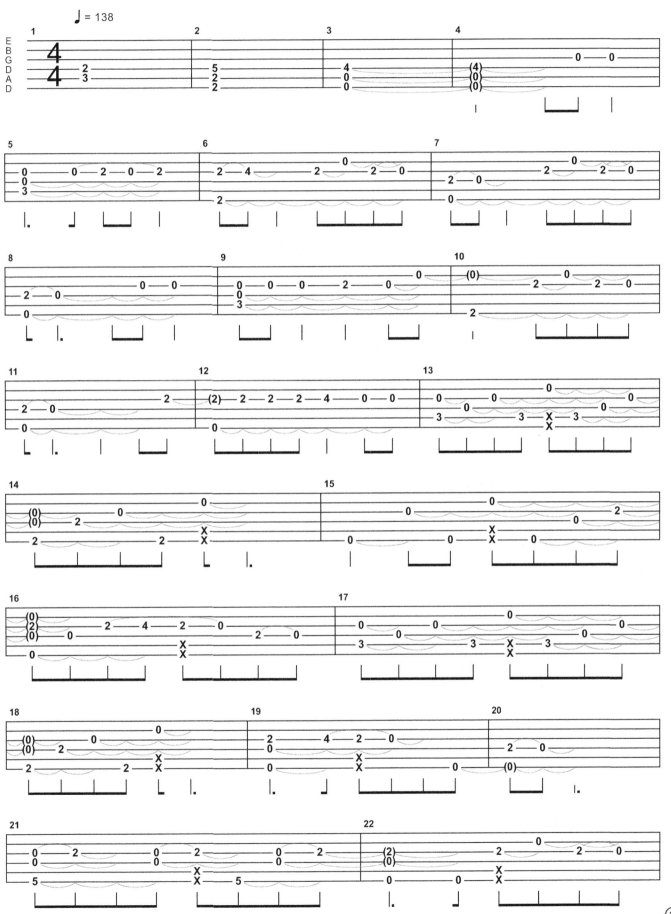

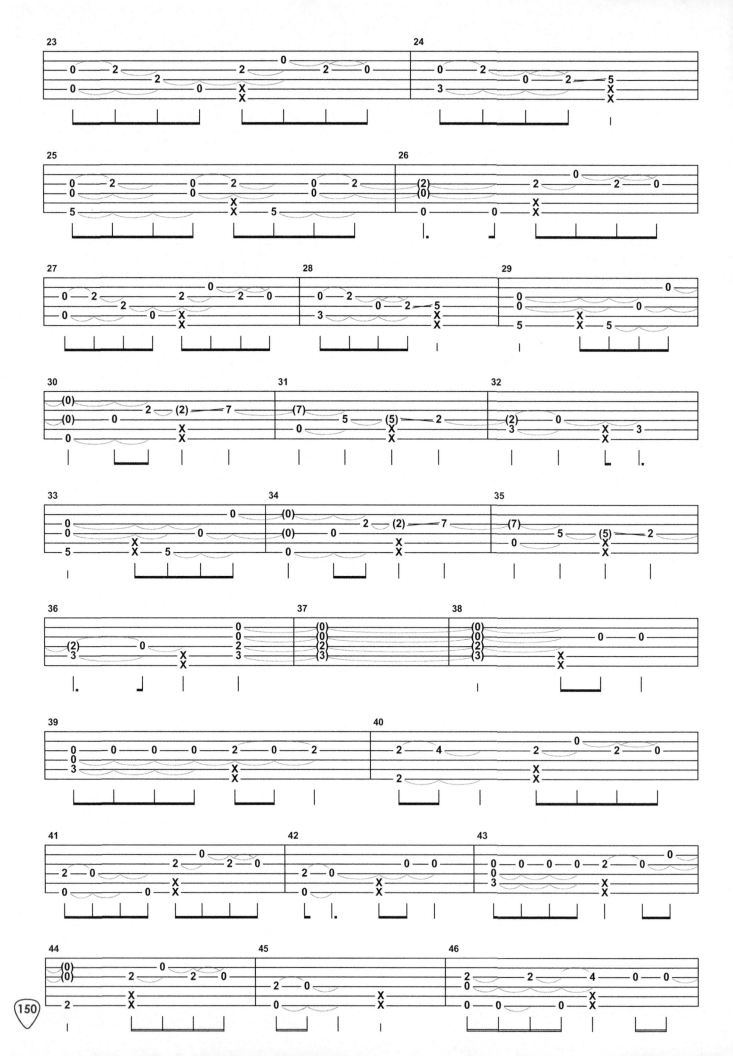

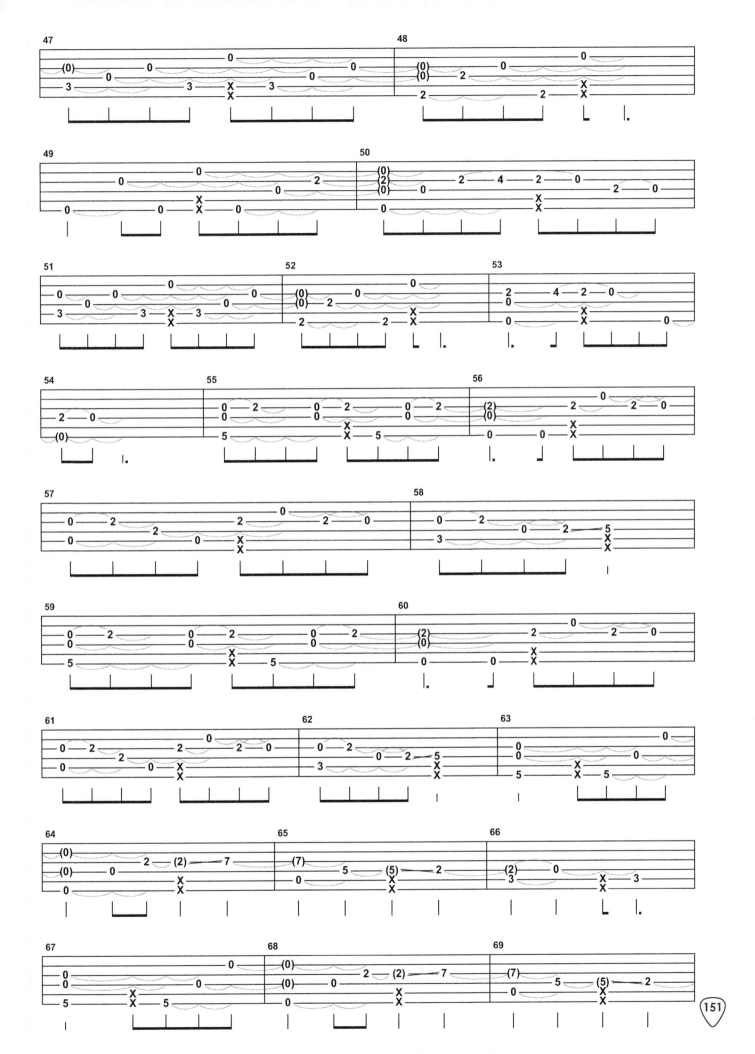

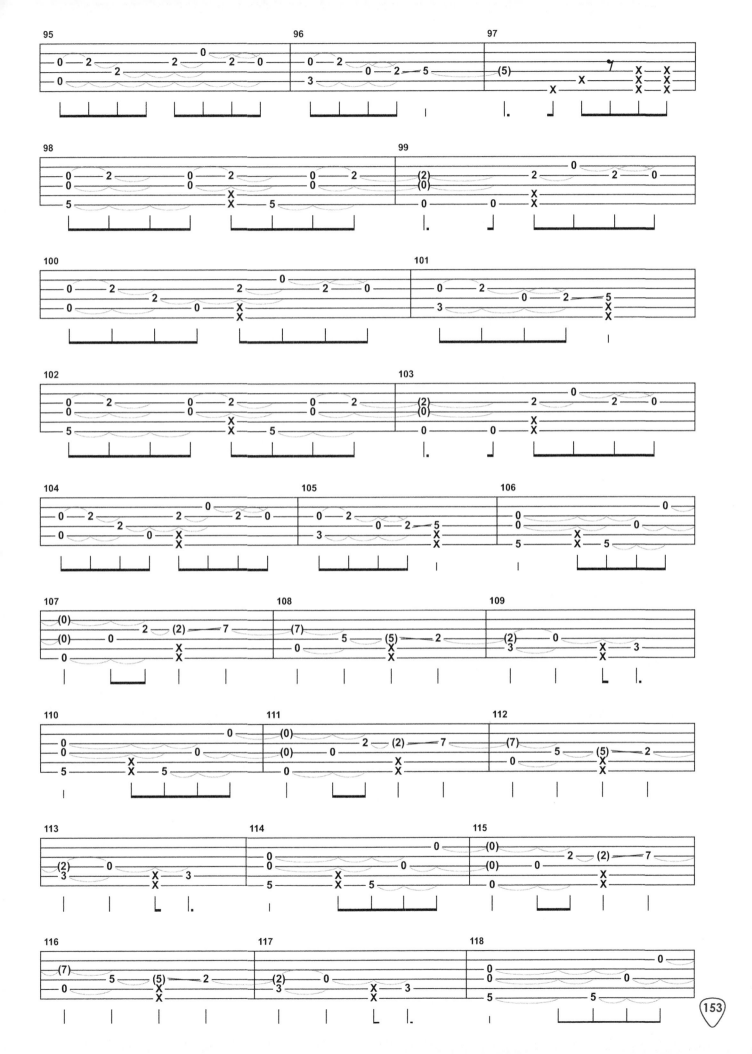

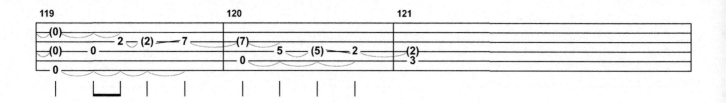

Taylor Swift
Red

Taylor Swift - Red (Fingerstyle Cover By Gp)

Track: Guitar - Acoustic Guitar (Steel)

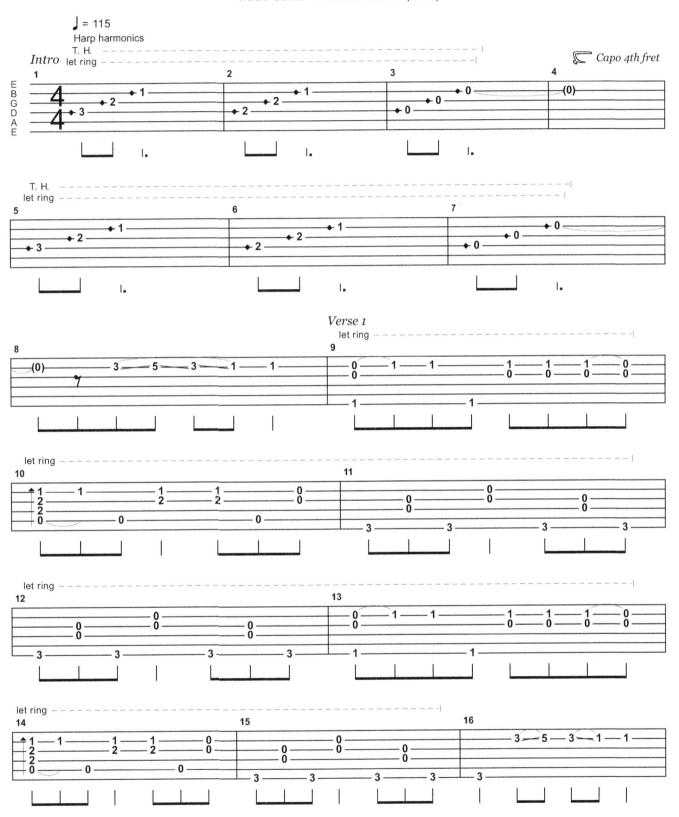

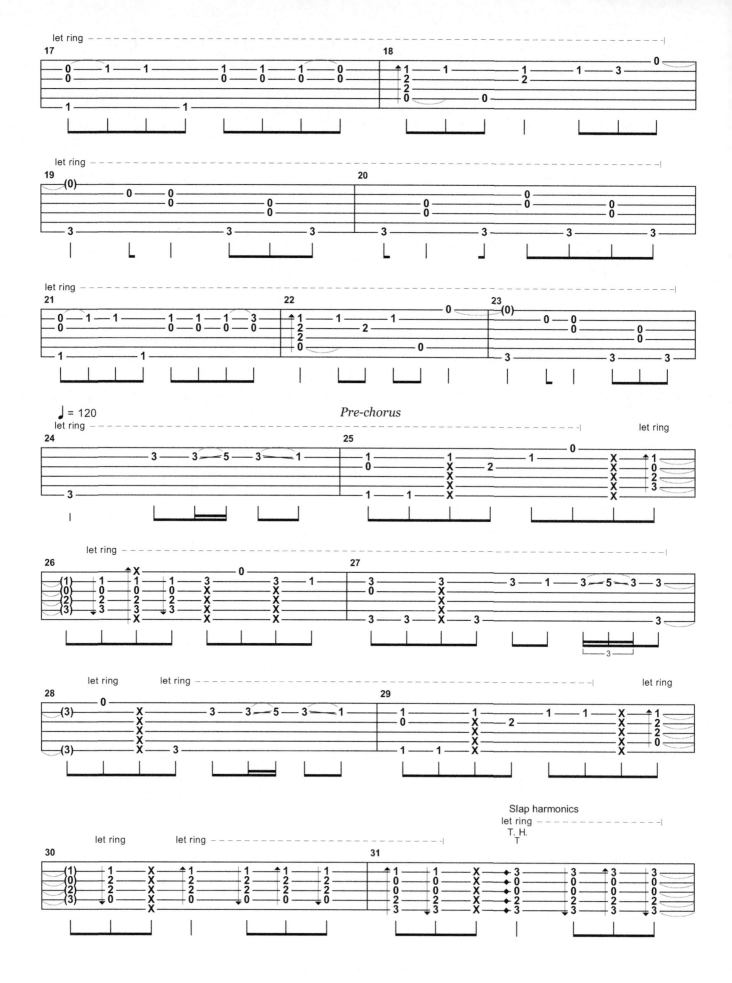

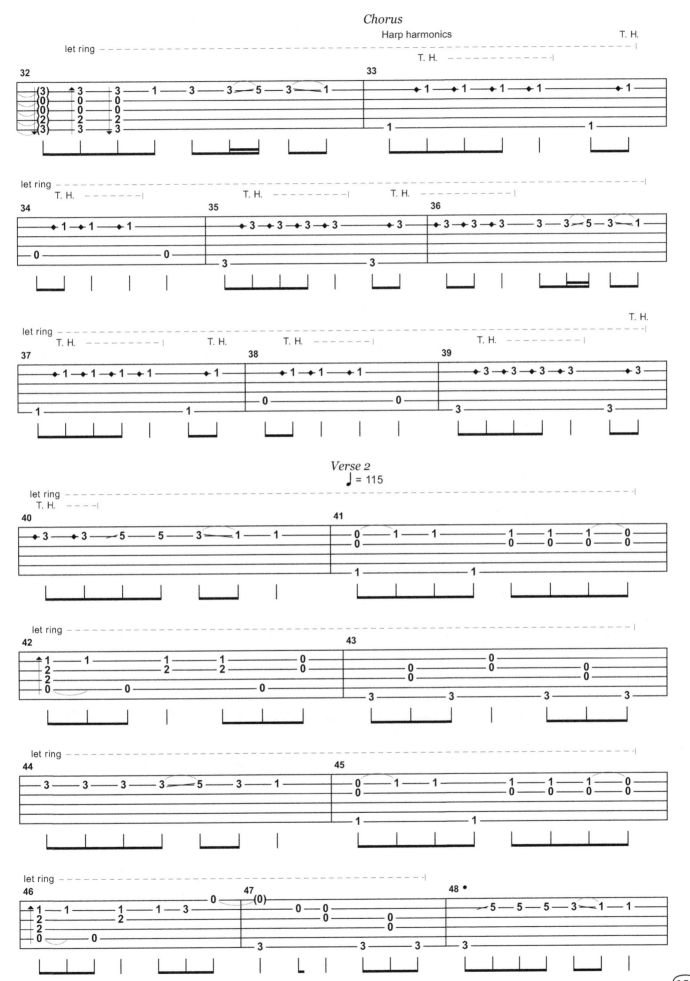

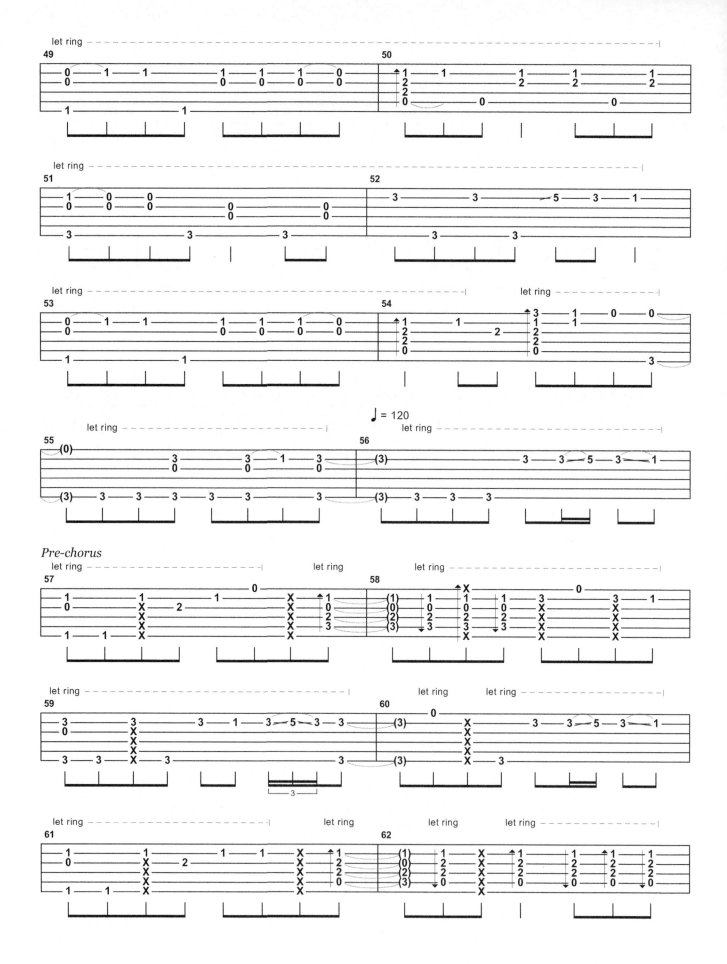

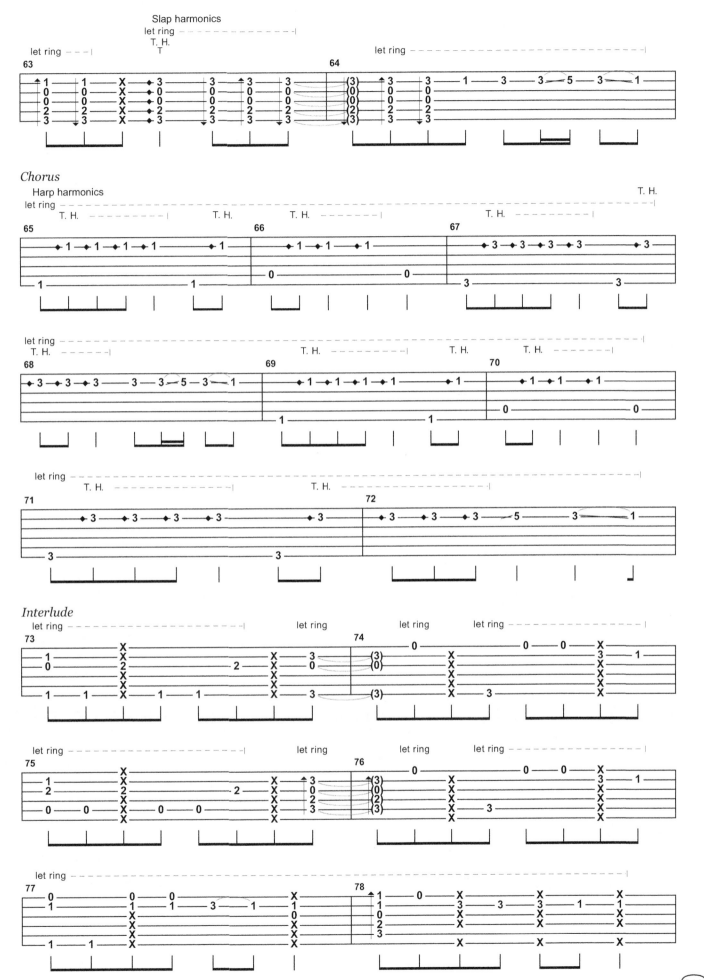

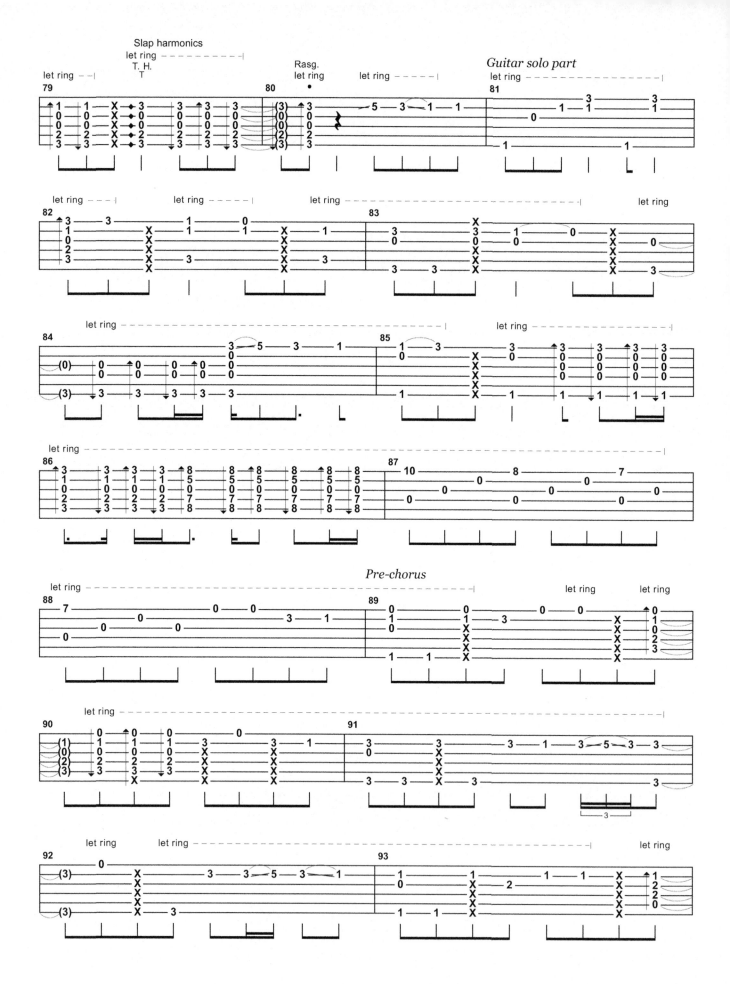

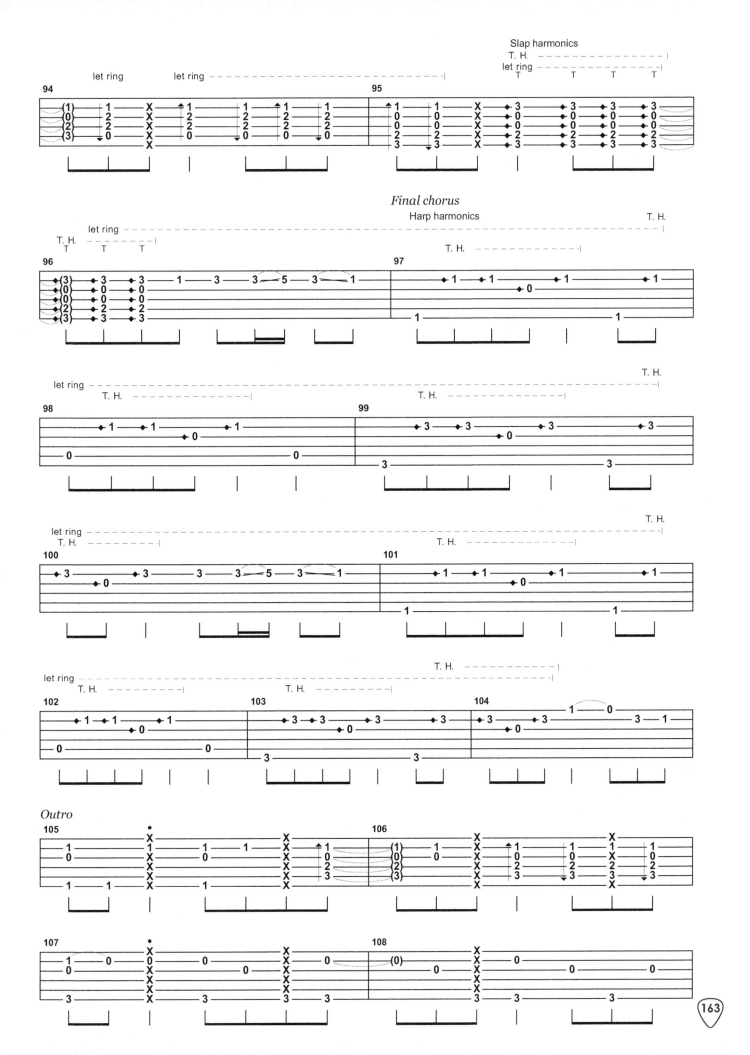

Final chorus

Outro

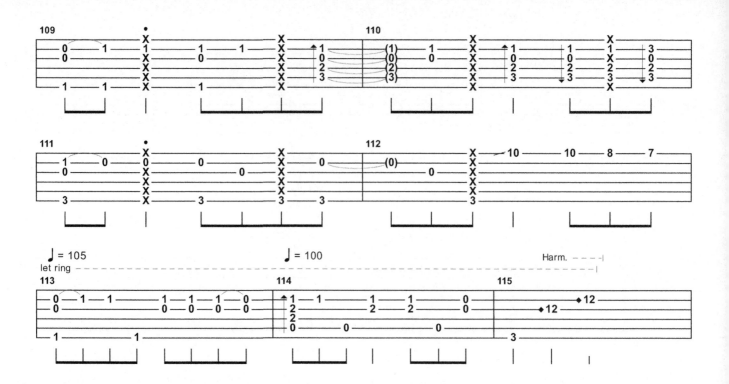

Taylor Swift
Enchanted

Taylor Swift - Enchanted (Speak Now Album)

Track: Track 1 - Acoustic Guitar (Steel)

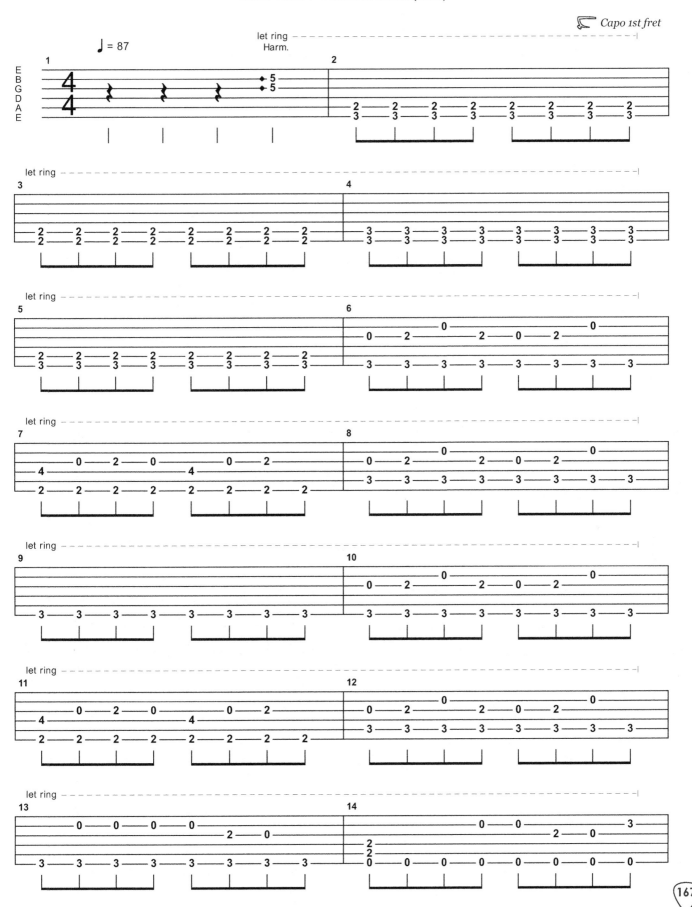

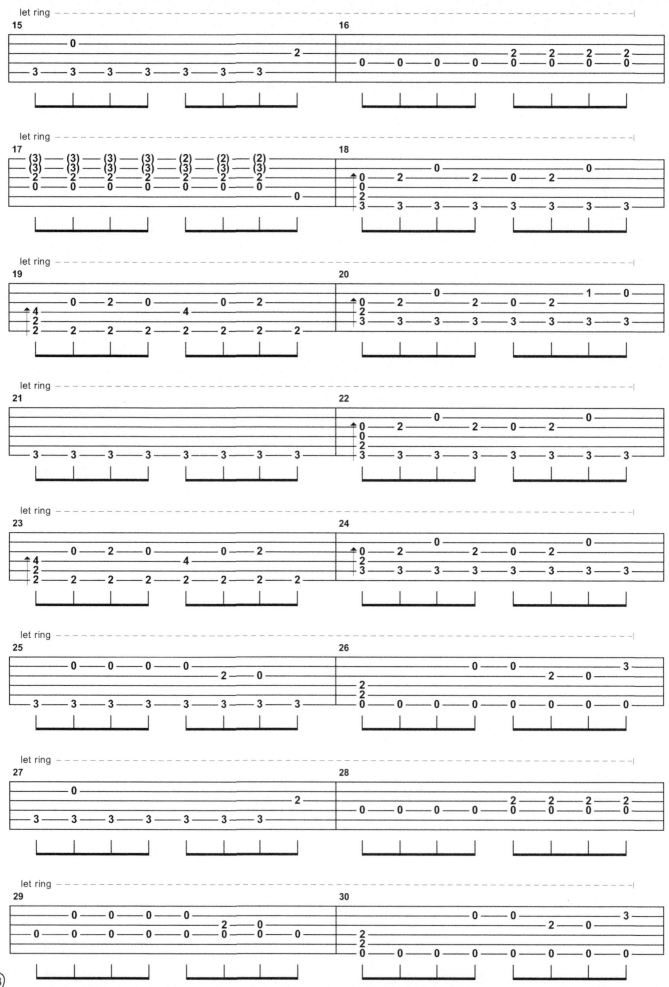

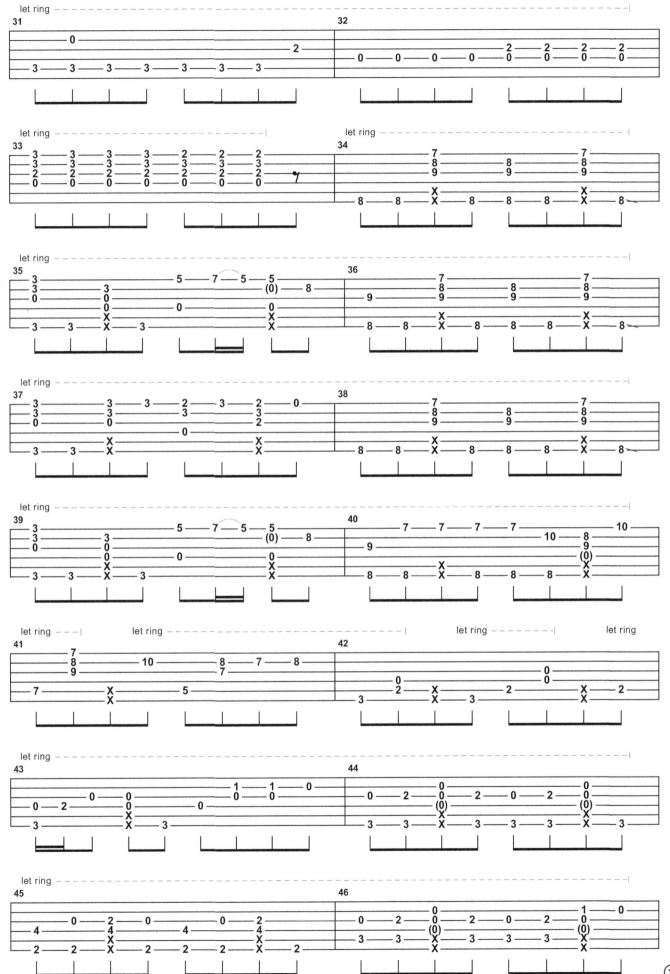

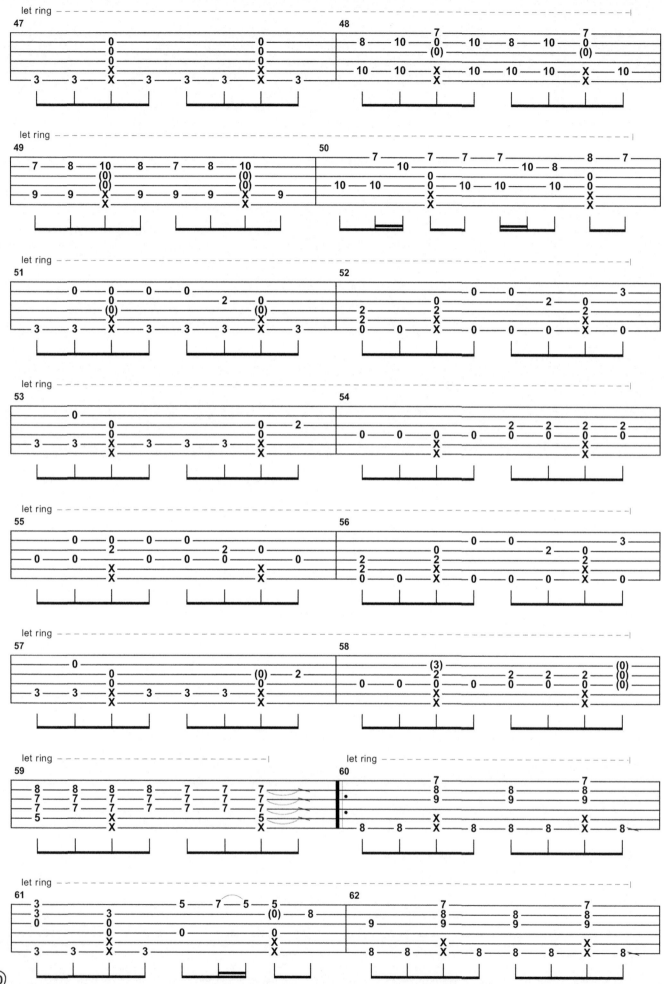

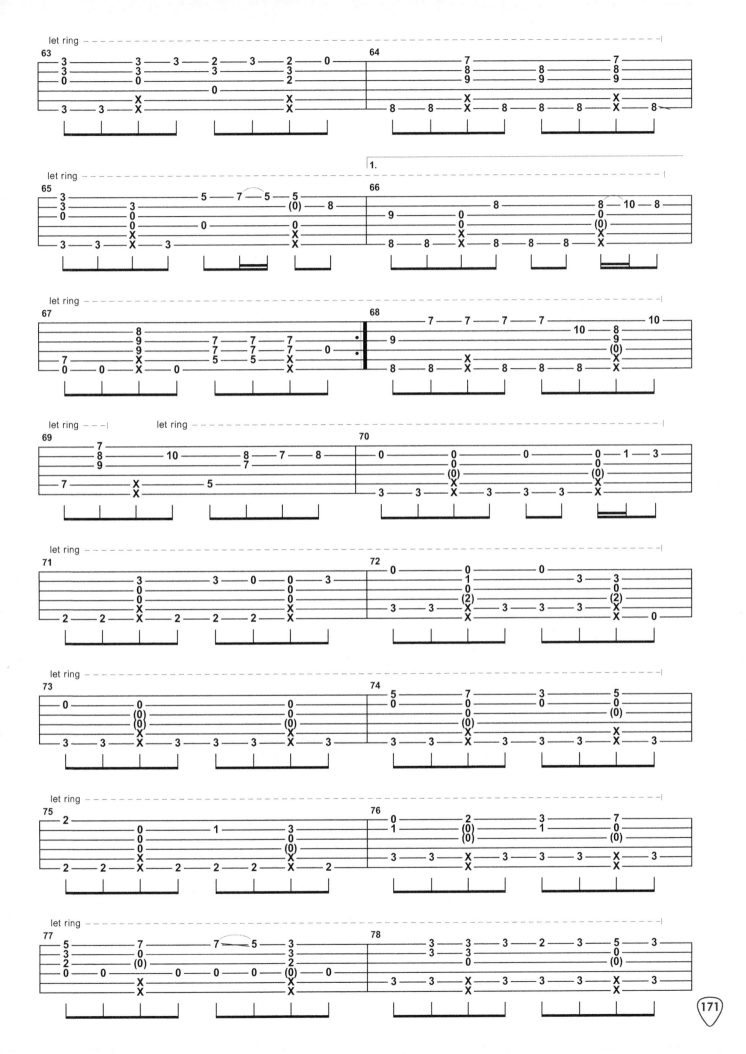

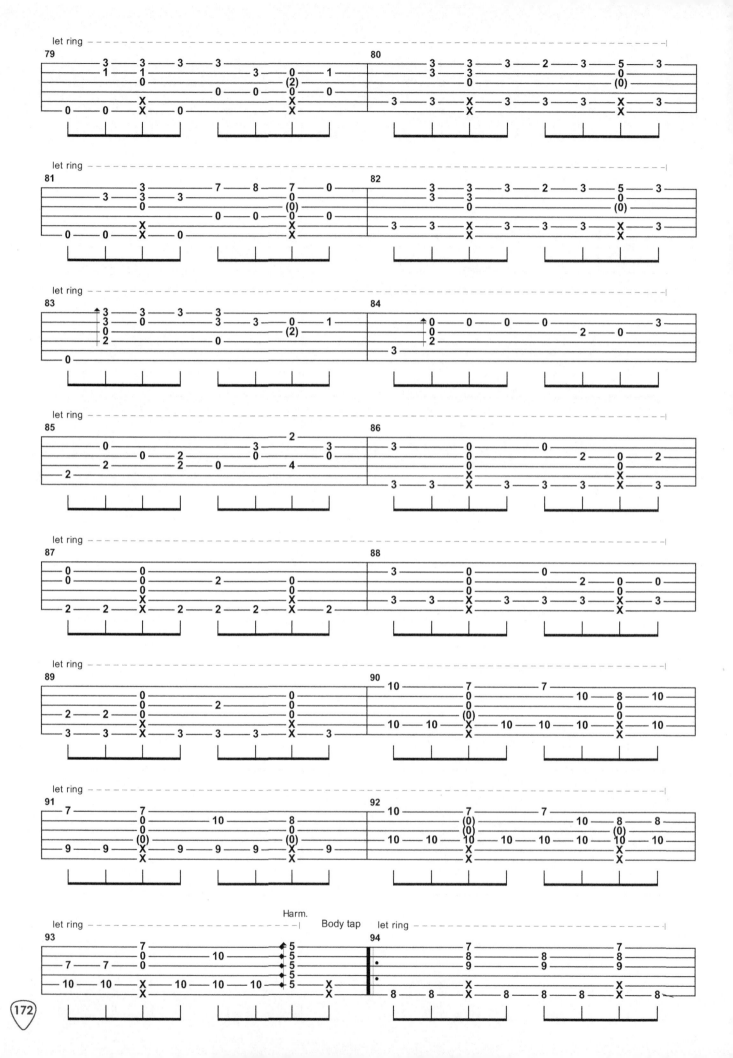

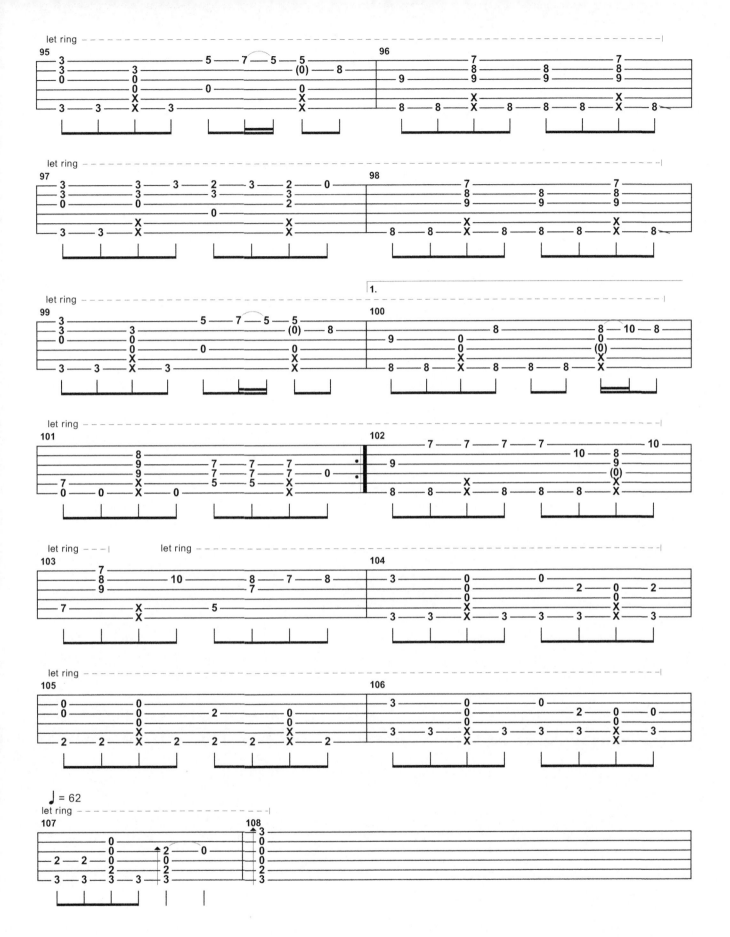

Taylor Swift
Spaks Fly

Taylor Swift - Sparks Fly

Track: Track 2 - Acoustic Guitar (Steel)

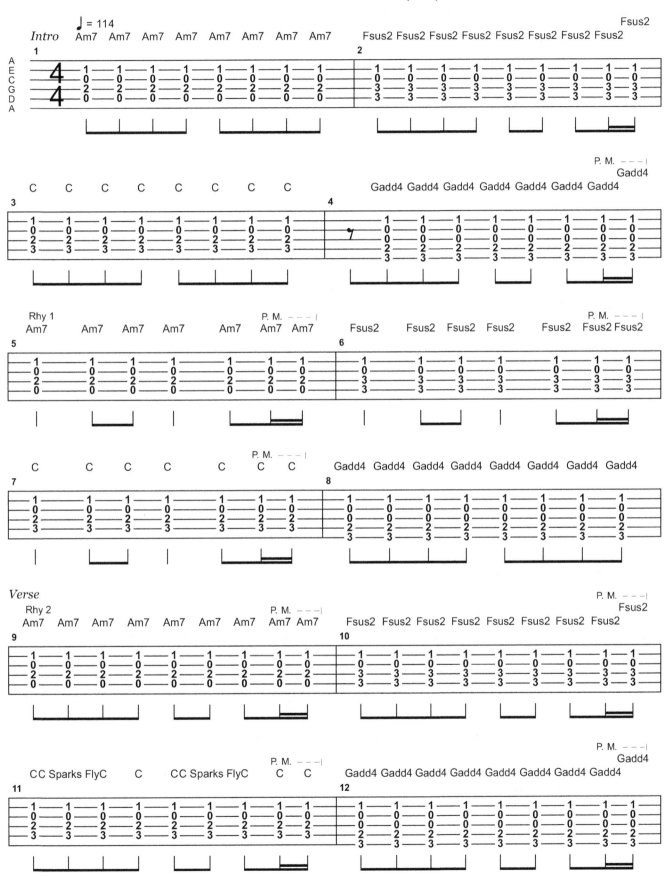

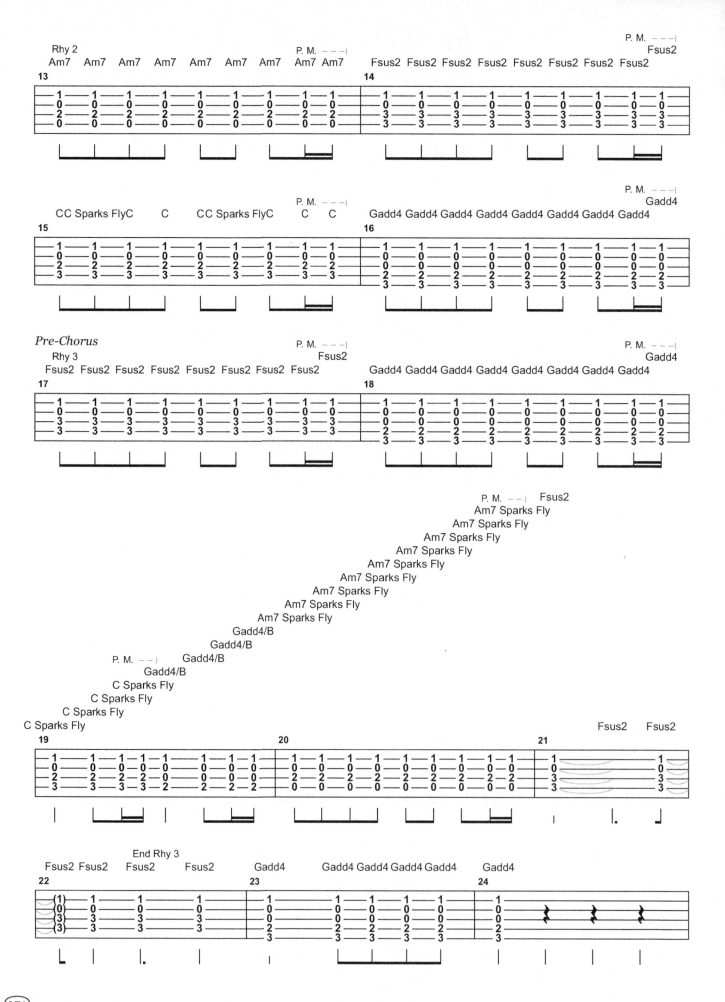

Chorus

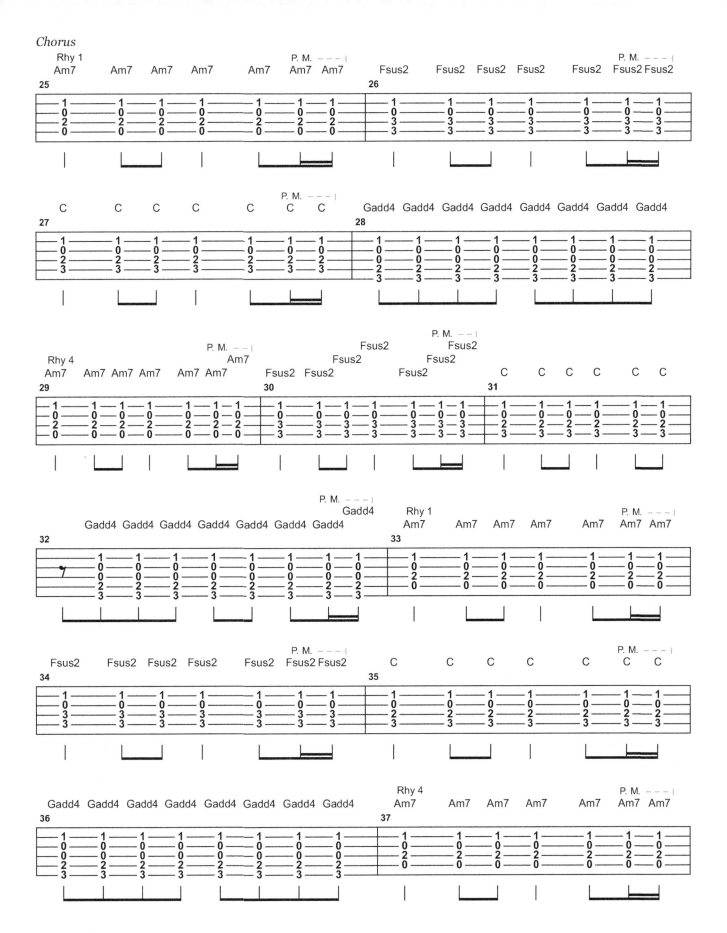

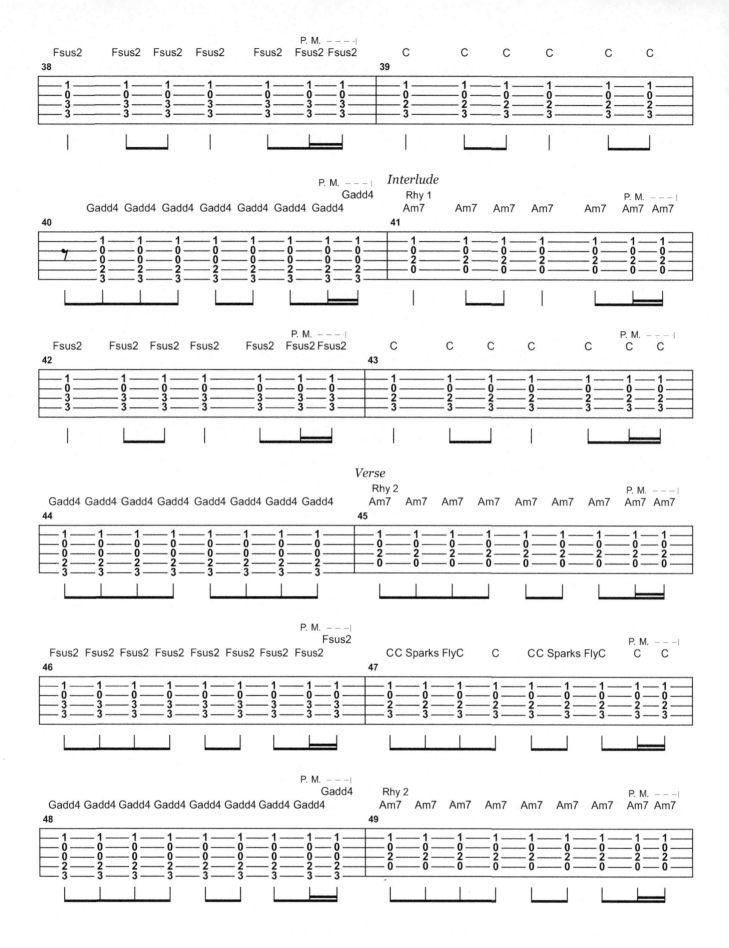

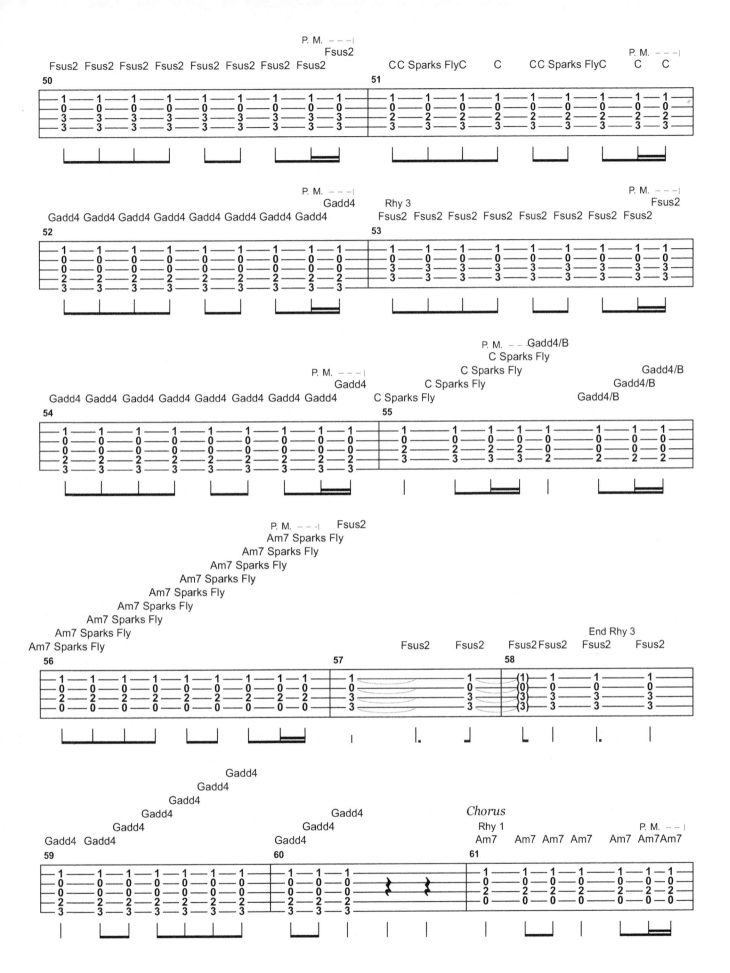

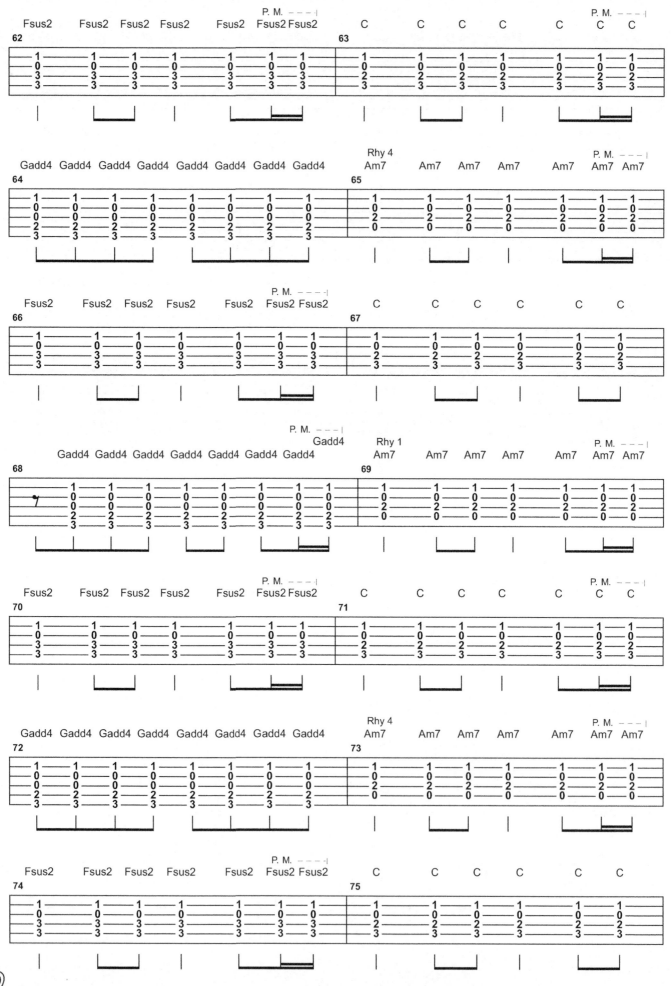

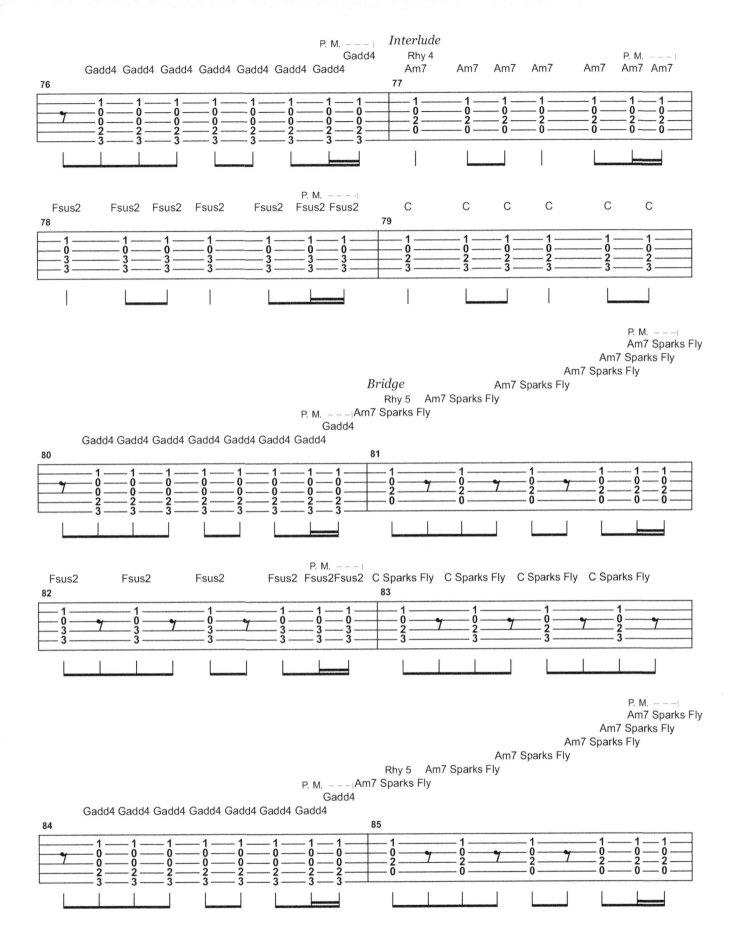

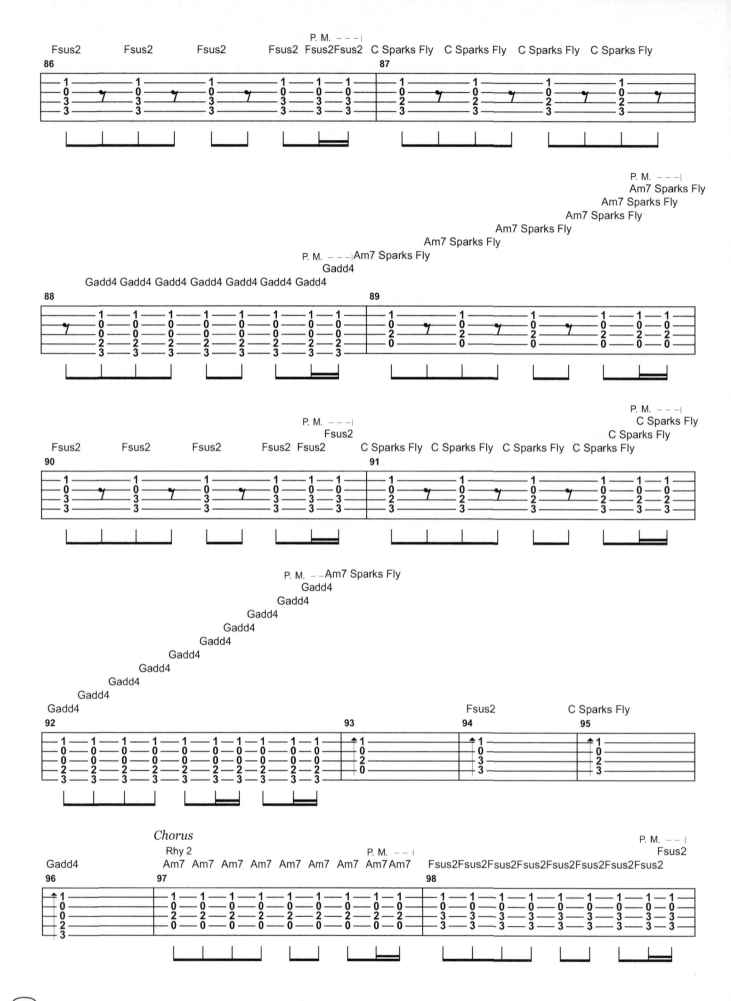

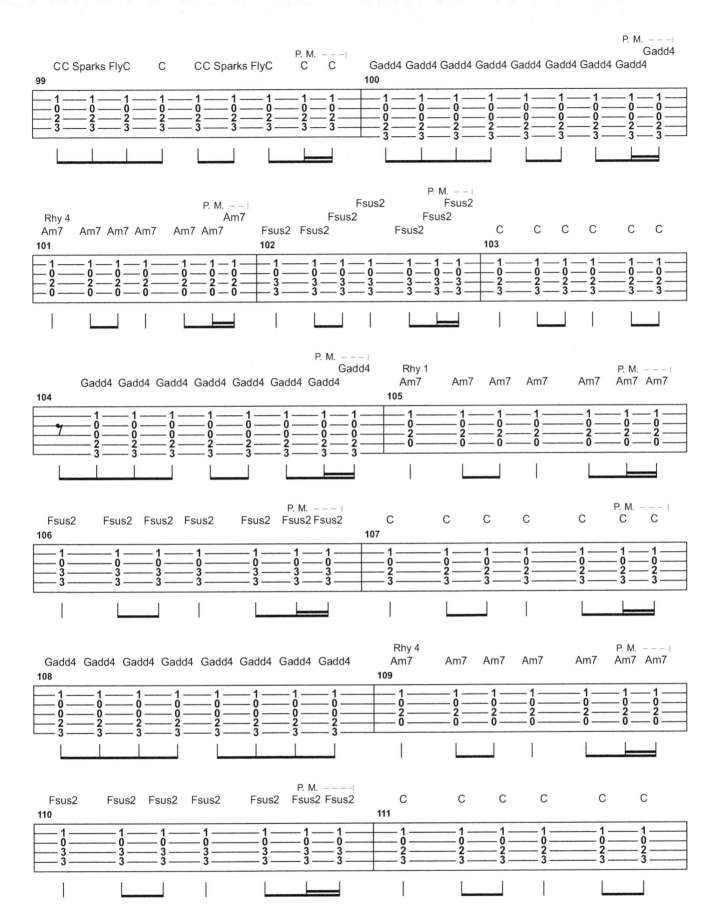

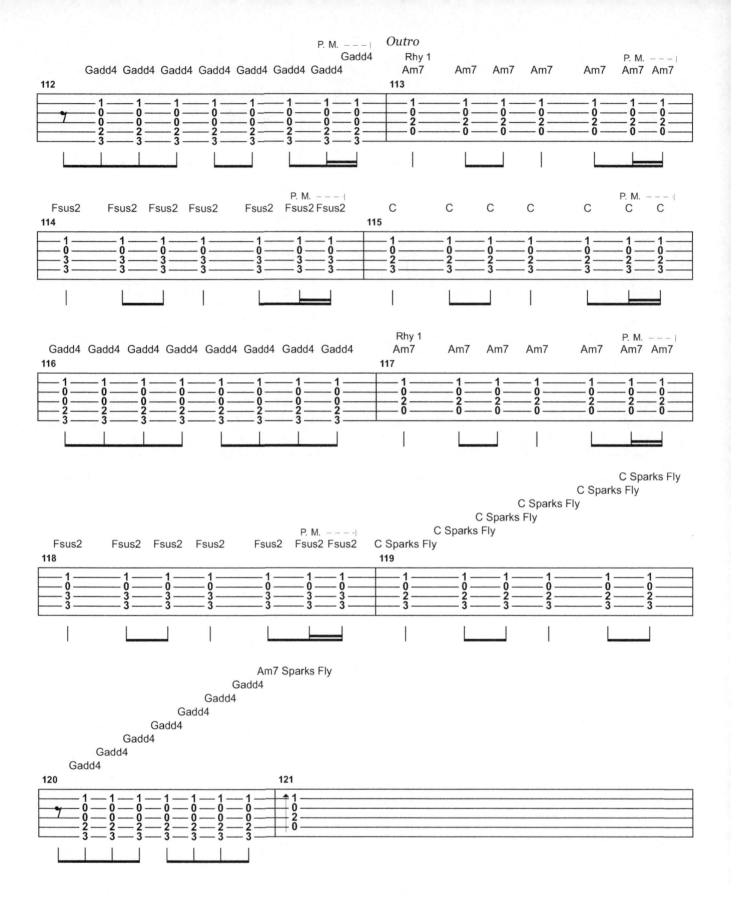

Taylor Swift
Treacherous

Taylor Swift - Treacherous

Track: Acoustic Guitar #1 - Acoustic Guitar (Nylon)

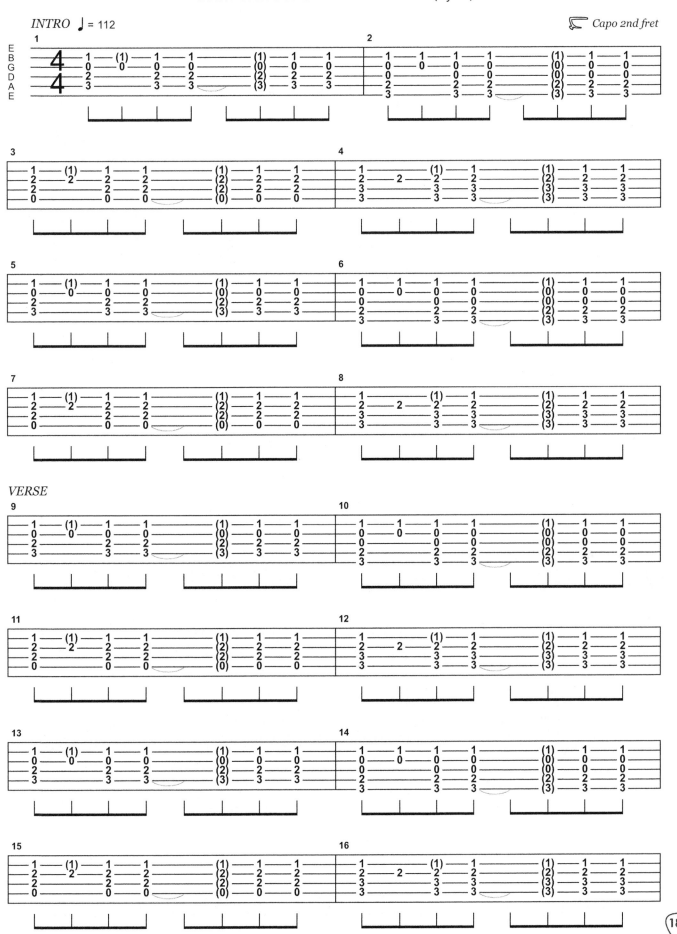

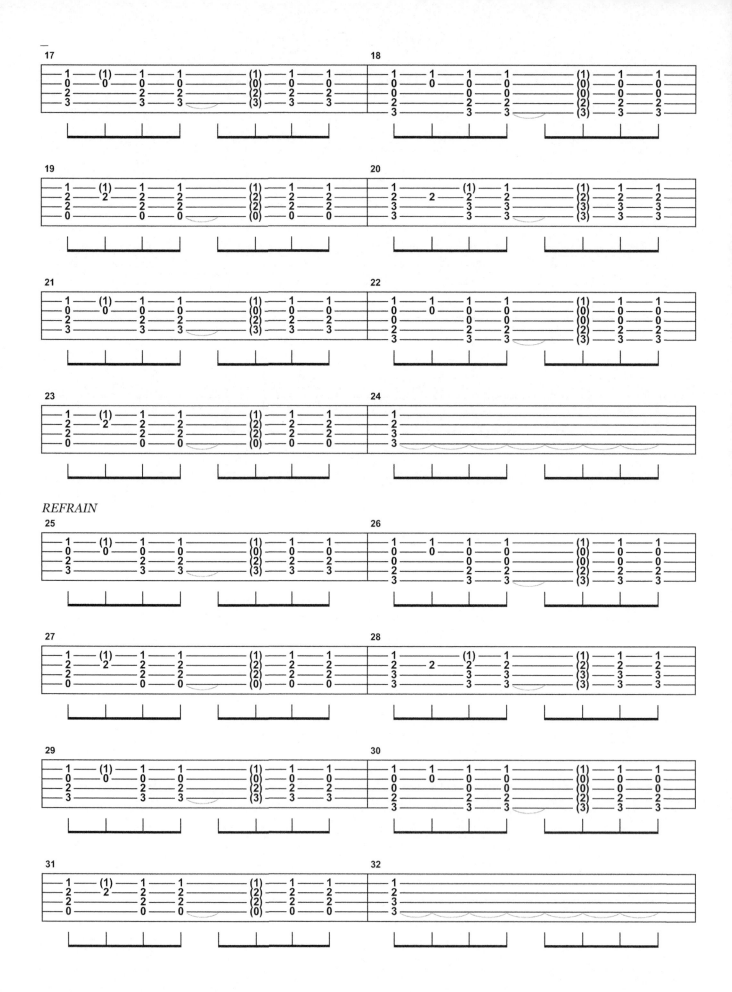

REFRAIN

INTER

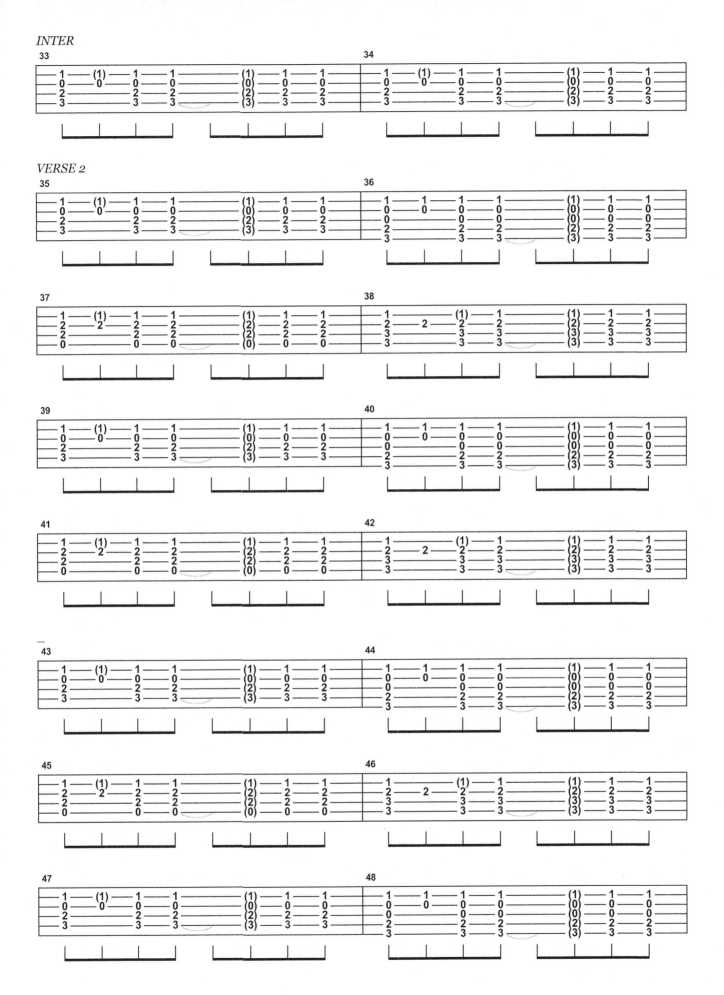

VERSE 2

189

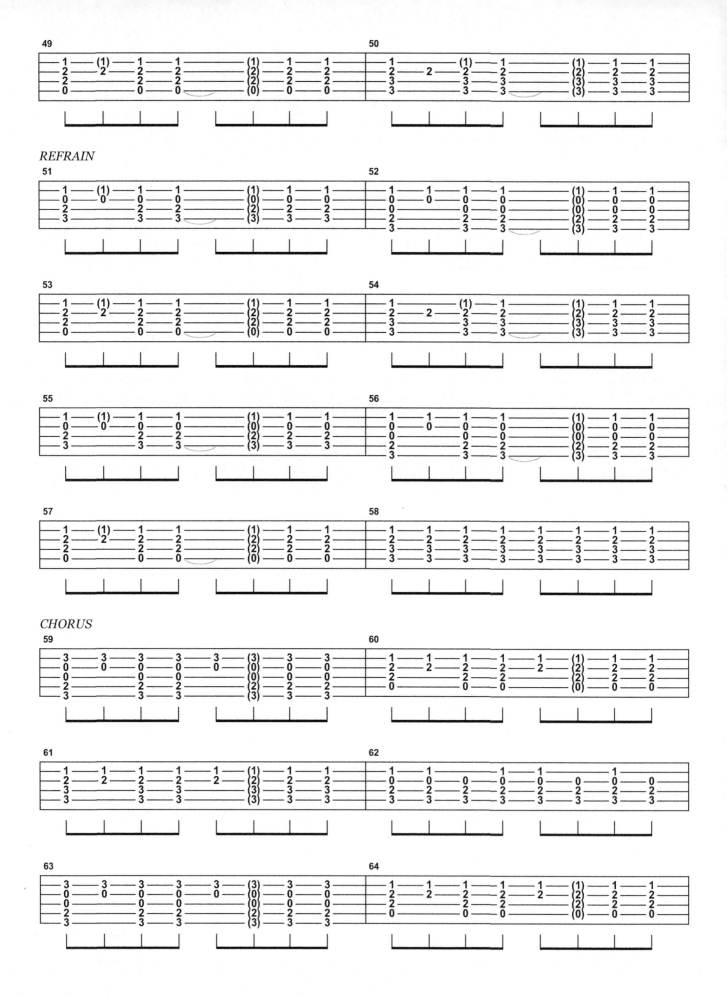

REFRAIN

CHORUS

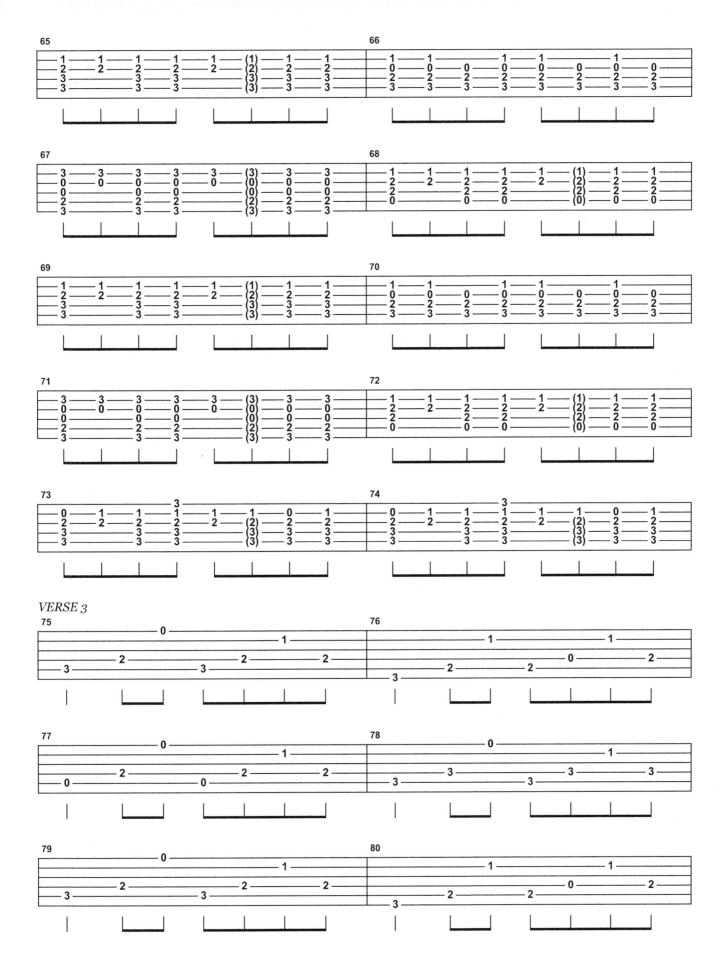

VERSE 3

BUILD UP

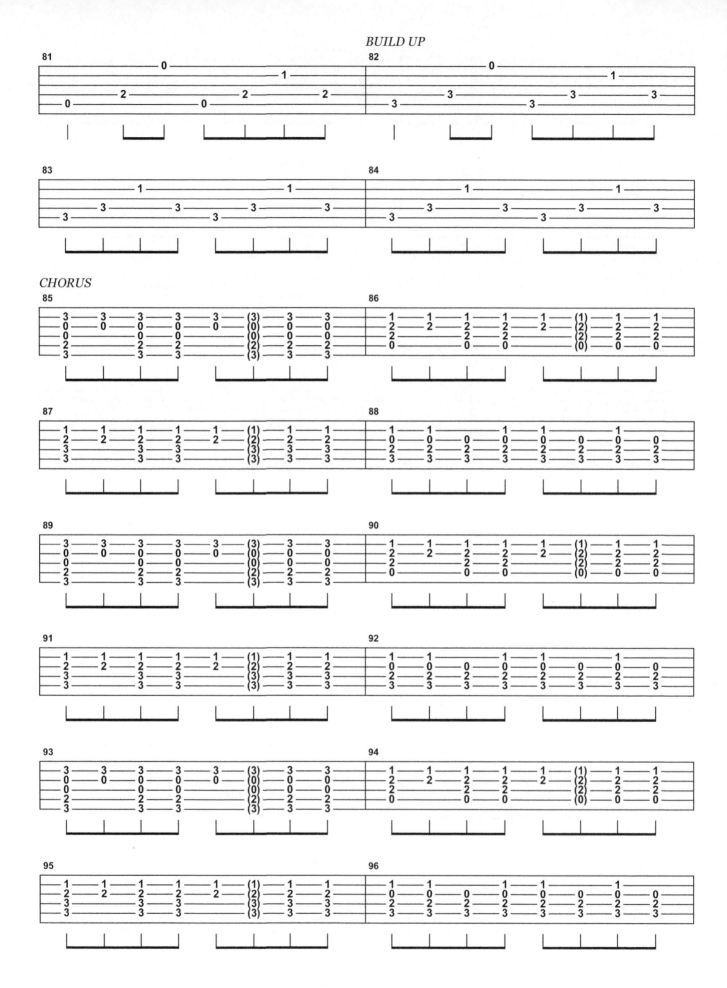

CHORUS

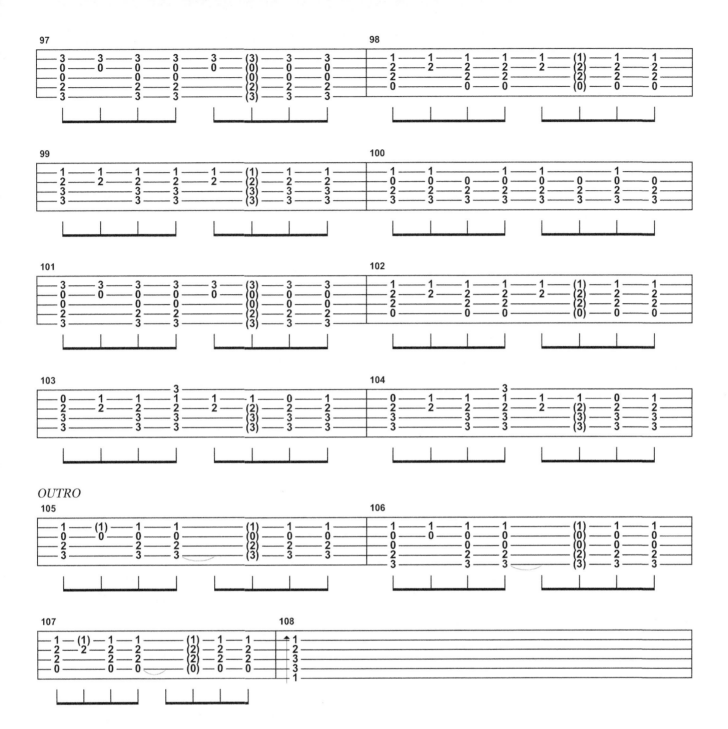

OUTRO

Taylor Swift - Treacherous

Track: Acoustic Guitar #2 - Acoustic Guitar (Steel)

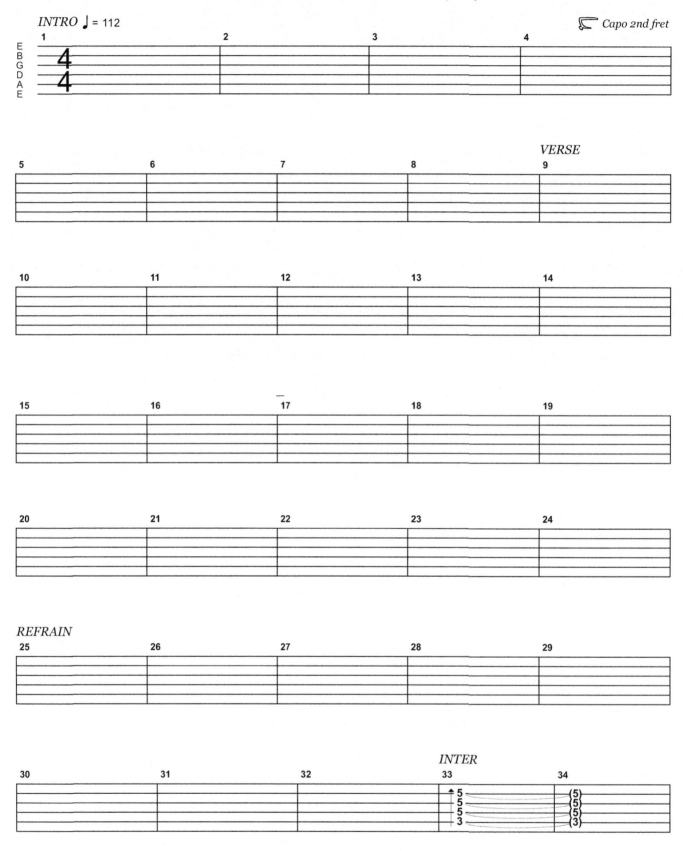

VERSE 2

35   36   37   38   39

40   41   42   43   44

45   46   47   48   49

REFRAIN

50   51   52   53   54

CHORUS

55   56   57   58   59

60   61   62   63   64

65   66   67   68   69

70   71   72   73   74

VERSE 3

75   76   77   78   79

BUILD UP

80   81   82

```
1 — 1 — 1 — 1 — 1 — 1 — 1 — 1
2 — 2 — 2 — 2 — 2 — 2 — 2 — 2
3 — 3 — 3 — 3 — 3 — 3 — 3 — 3
3 — 3 — 3 — 3 — 3 — 3 — 3 — 3
```

83   84

```
1 — 1 — 1 — 1 — 1 — 1 — 1 — 1     1 — 1 — 1 — 1 — 1 — 1 — 1 — 1
2 — 2 — 2 — 2 — 2 — 2 — 2 — 2     2 — 2 — 2 — 2 — 2 — 2 — 2 — 2
3 — 3 — 3 — 3 — 3 — 3 — 3 — 3     3 — 3 — 3 — 3 — 3 — 3 — 3 — 3
3 — 3 — 3 — 3 — 3 — 3 — 3 — 3     3 — 3 — 3 — 3 — 3 — 3 — 3 — 3
```

CHORUS

85   86

```
3 — 3 — 3 — 3 — 3 — (3) — 3 — 3     1 — 1 — 1 — 1 — 1 — (1) — 1 — 1
0 — 0 — 0 — 0 — 0 — (0) — 0 — 0     2 — 2 — 2 — 2 — 2 — (2) — 2 — 2
0 —   — 0 —   — 0 — (0) — 0 — 0     2 —   — 2 —   — 2 — (2) — 2 — 2
2 —   — 2 — 2 —   — (2) — 2 — 2     0 —   —   — 0 —   — (0) — 0 — 0
3 —   — 3 — 3 —   — (3) — 3 — 3
```

87   88

```
1 — 1 — 1 — 1 — 1 — (1) — 1 — 1     1 — 1 —   — 1 — 1 —   — 1 —
2 — 2 — 2 — 2 — 2 — (2) — 2 — 2     0 — 0 — 0 — 0 — 0 — 0 — 0 — 0
3 —   — 3 — 3 —   — (3) — 3 — 3     2 — 2 — 2 — 2 — 2 — 2 — 2 — 2
3 —   — 3 — 3 —   — (3) — 3 — 3     3 — 3 — 3 — 3 — 3 — 3 — 3 — 3
```

89   90

```
3 — 3 — 3 — 3 — 3 — (3) — 3 — 3     1 — 1 — 1 — 1 — 1 — (1) — 1 — 1
0 — 0 — 0 — 0 — 0 — (0) — 0 — 0     2 — 2 — 2 — 2 — 2 — (2) — 2 — 2
0 —   — 0 —   — 0 — (0) — 0 — 0     2 —   — 2 —   — 2 — (2) — 2 — 2
2 —   — 2 — 2 —   — (2) — 2 — 2     0 —   —   — 0 —   — (0) — 0 — 0
3 —   — 3 — 3 —   — (3) — 3 — 3
```

91   92

```
1 — 1 — 1 — 1 — 1 — (1) — 1 — 1     1 — 1 —   — 1 — 1 —   — 1 —
2 — 2 — 2 — 2 — 2 — (2) — 2 — 2     0 — 0 — 0 — 0 — 0 — 0 — 0 — 0
3 —   — 3 — 3 —   — (3) — 3 — 3     2 — 2 — 2 — 2 — 2 — 2 — 2 — 2
3 —   — 3 — 3 —   — (3) — 3 — 3     3 — 3 — 3 — 3 — 3 — 3 — 3 — 3
```

93   94

```
3 — 3 — 3 — 3 — 3 — (3) — 3 — 3     1 — 1 — 1 — 1 — 1 — (1) — 1 — 1
0 — 0 — 0 — 0 — 0 — (0) — 0 — 0     2 — 2 — 2 — 2 — 2 — (2) — 2 — 2
0 —   — 0 —   — 0 — (0) — 0 — 0     2 —   — 2 —   — 2 — (2) — 2 — 2
2 —   — 2 — 2 —   — (2) — 2 — 2     0 —   —   — 0 —   — (0) — 0 — 0
3 —   — 3 — 3 —   — (3) — 3 — 3
```

196

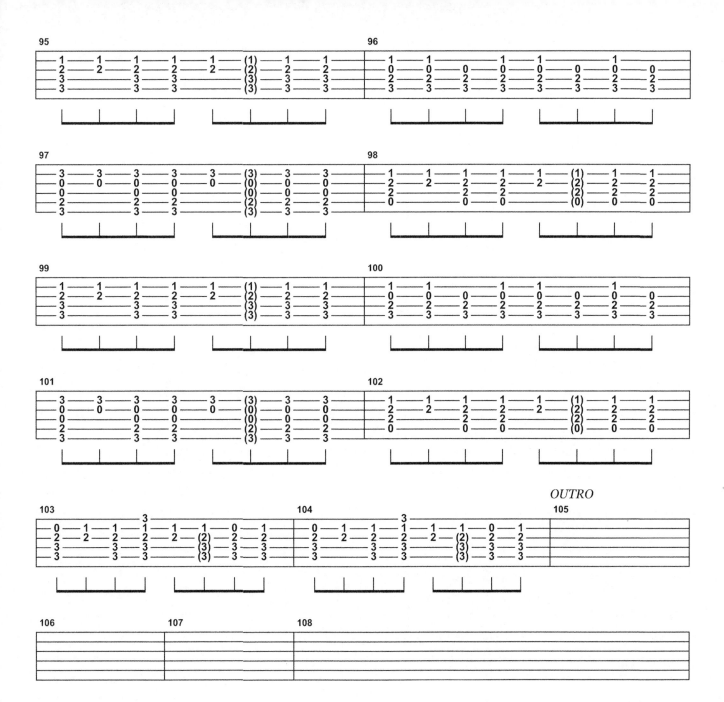

Taylor Swift

Ours

Taylor Swift - Ours

Track: Pista 1 - Acoustic Guitar (Steel)

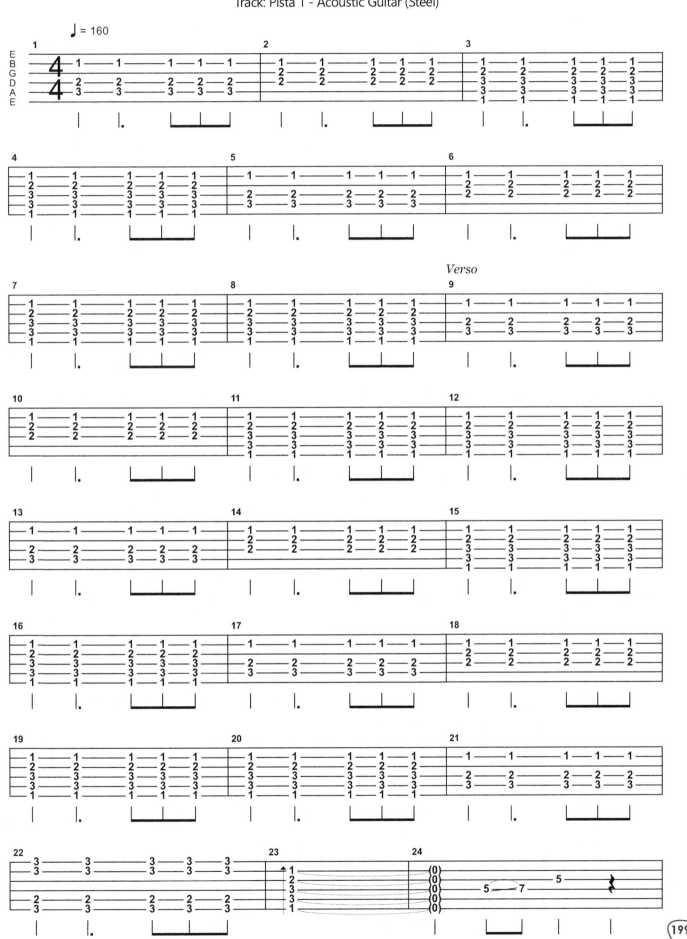

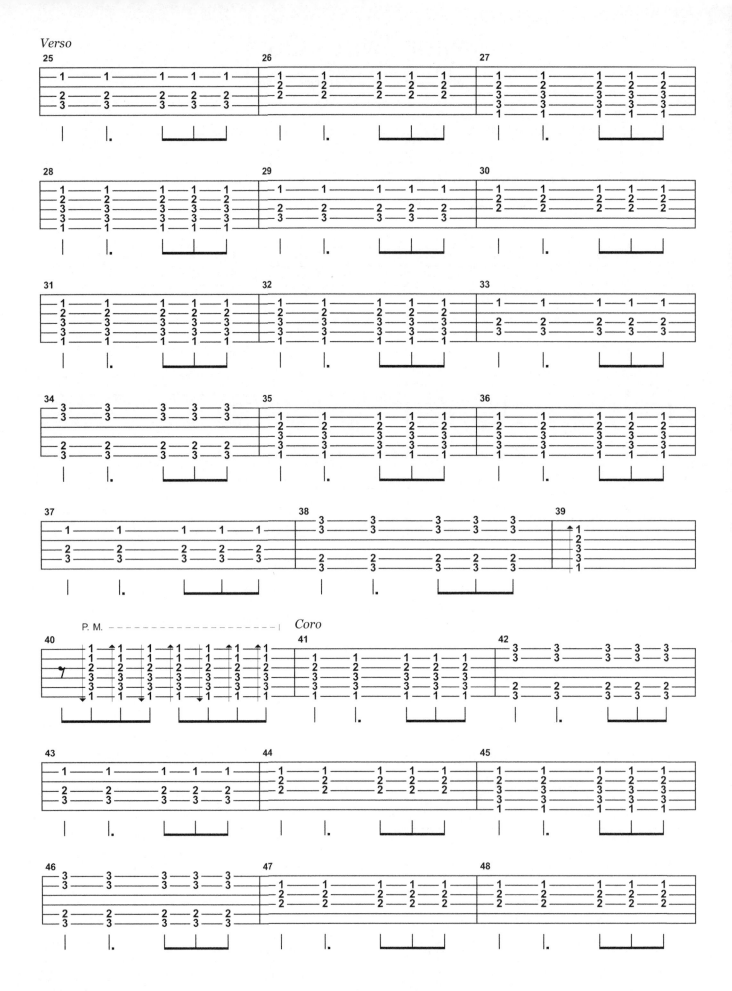

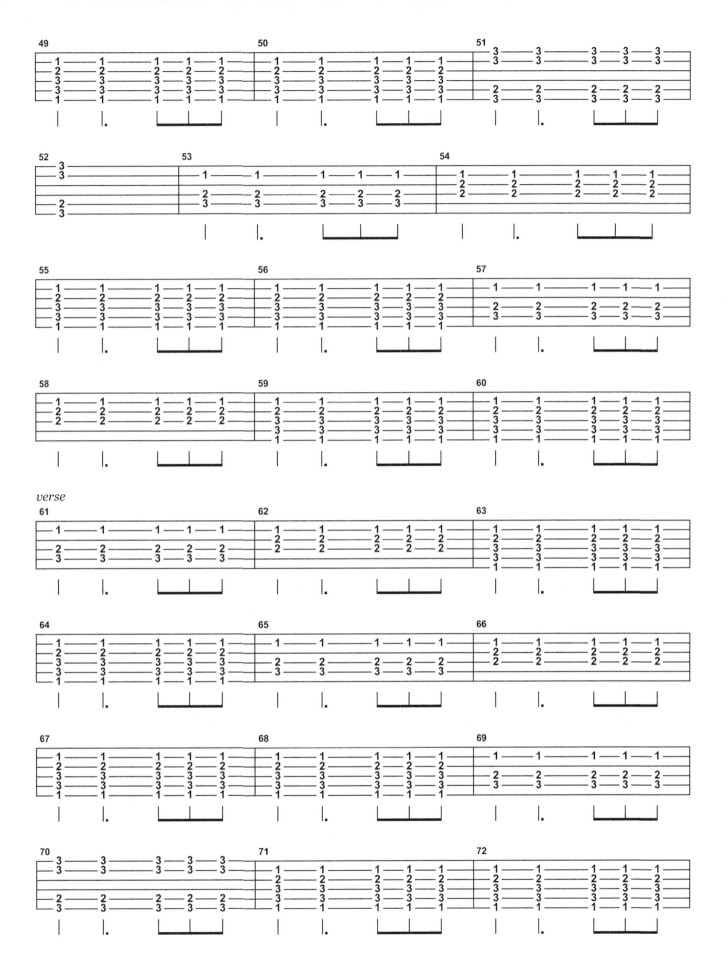

verse

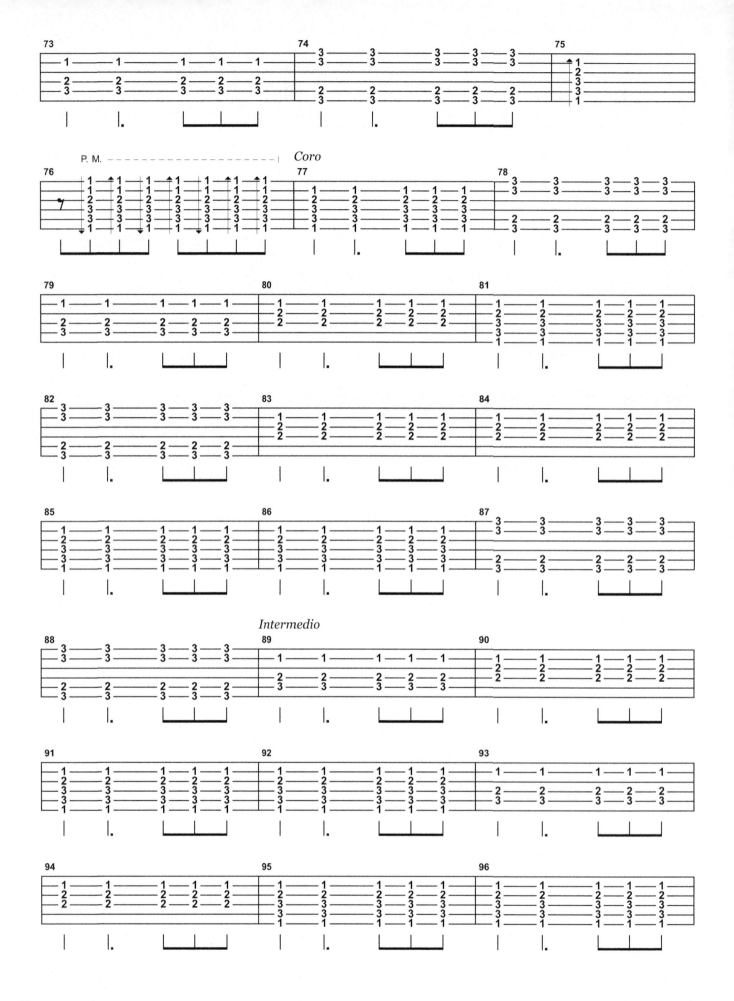

Puente

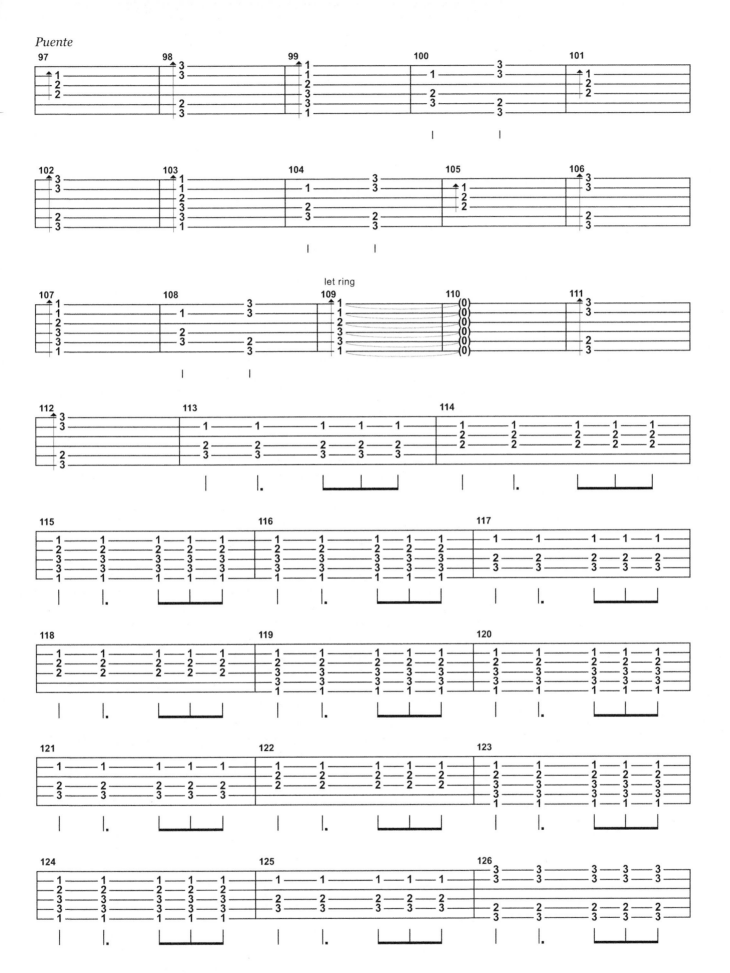

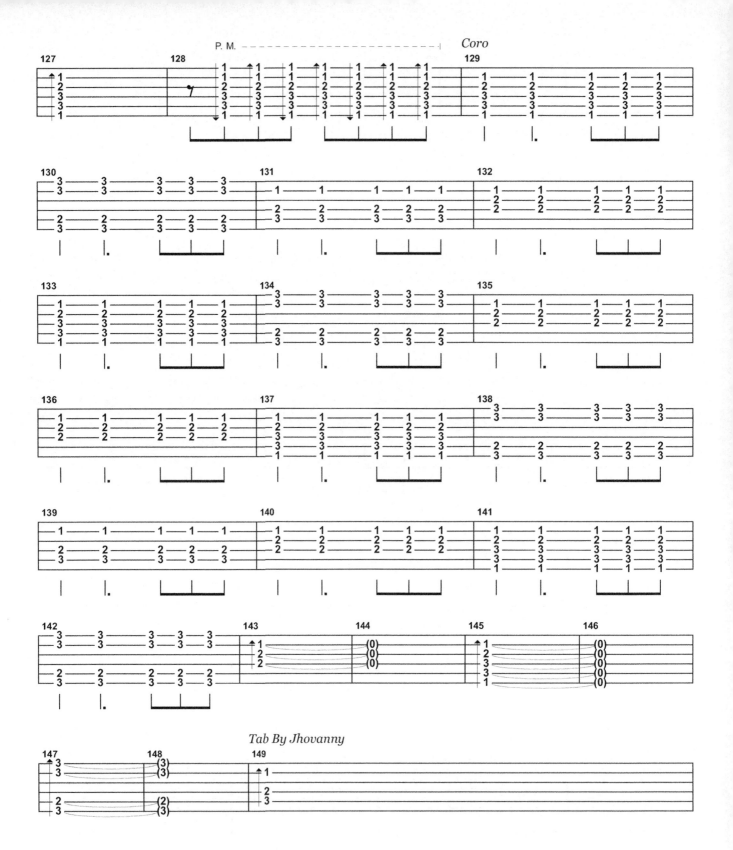

P. M. -| *Coro*

Tab By Jhovanny

Taylor Swift

Christmas Tree Farm

Taylor Swift - Christmas Tree Farm

Track: Guitar - Acoustic Guitar (Steel)

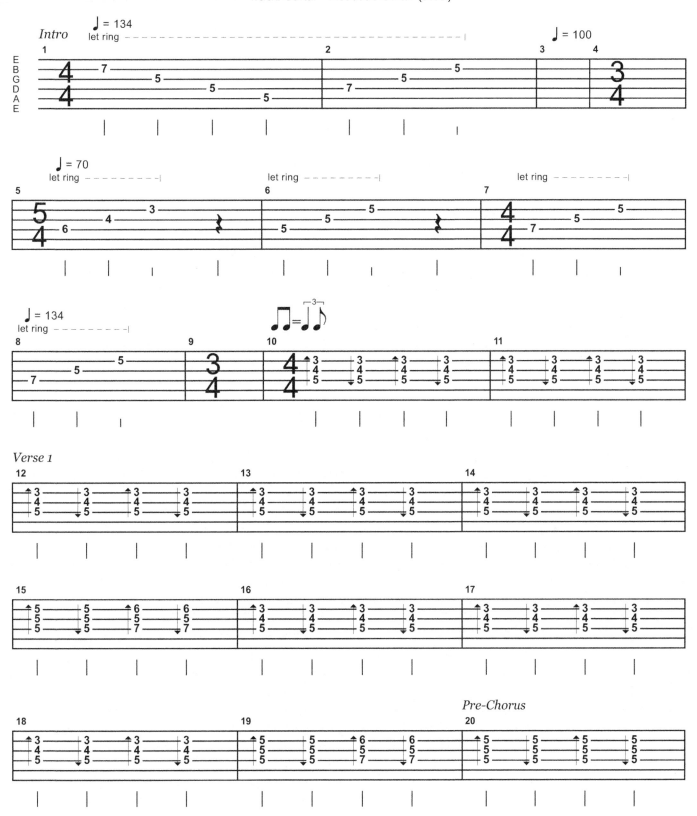

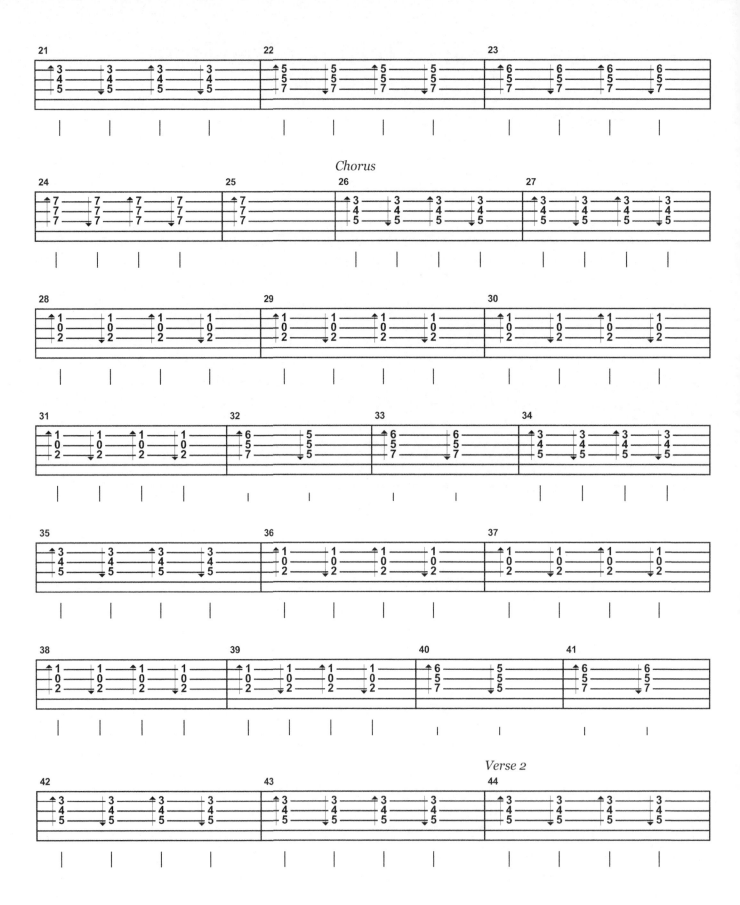

Chorus

Verse 2

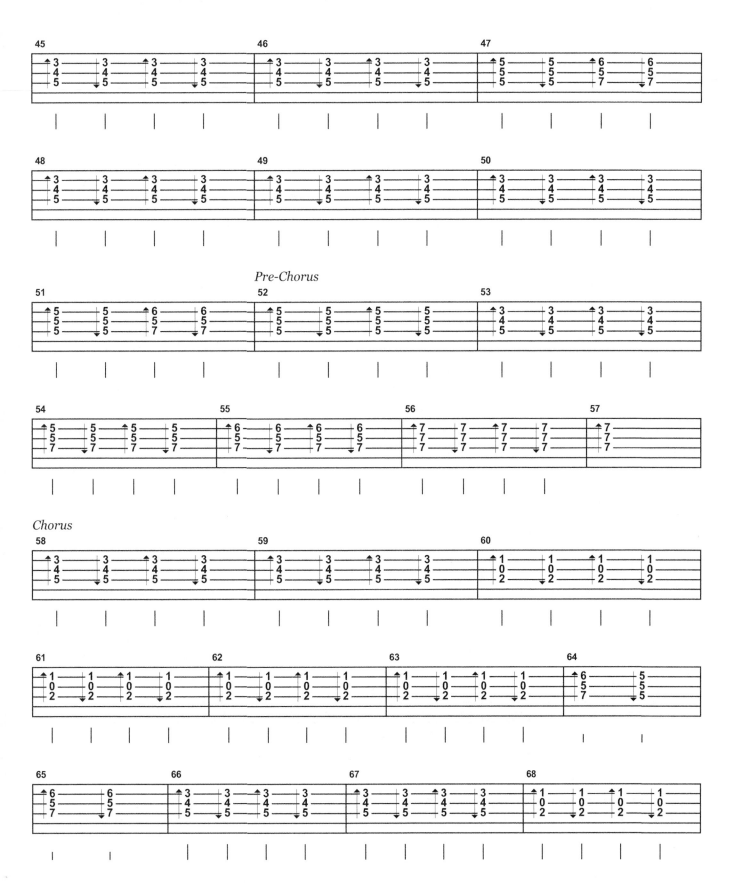

Pre-Chorus

Chorus

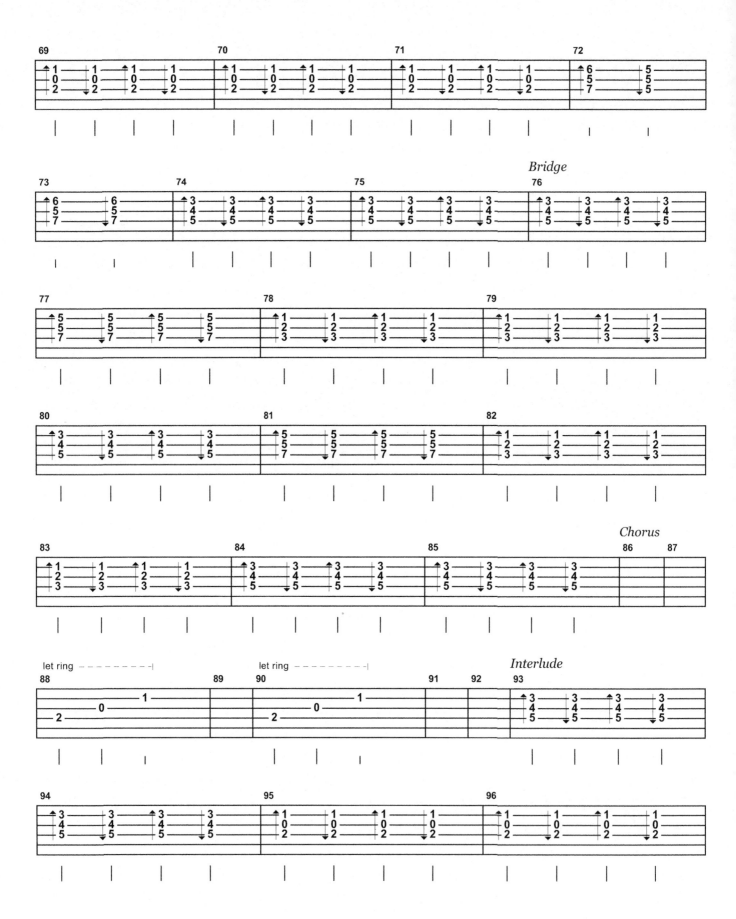

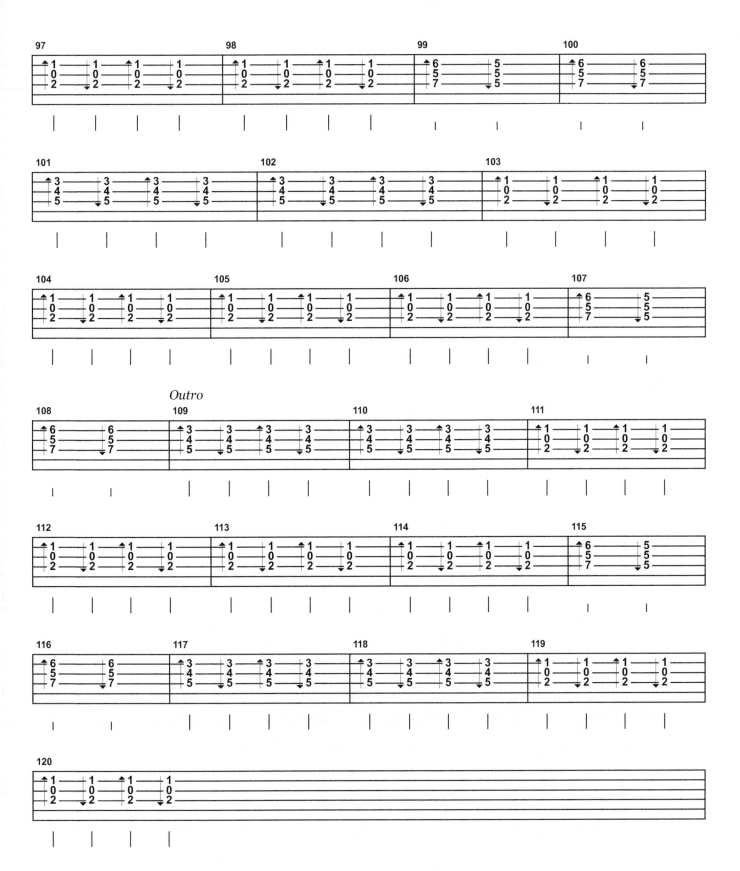

Outro

Thank You!

Thank you for choosing Taylor Swift Guitar Tab Book! We hope you've enjoyed playing and mastering the iconic songs of Taylor Swift. Your support means the world to us, and we're thrilled to be a part of your musical journey.

If you've found this book helpful and inspiring, we invite you to explore our other related books that cater to your passion for music. Whether you're a Taylor Swift enthusiast or eager to dive into the world of guitar playing, our collection has something for every music lover.